I0050456

ECONOMIC HISTORY

A LIVERPOOL MERCHANT HOUSE

BUSINESS HISTORY

A LIVERPOOL MERCHANT HOUSE

Being the history of Alfred Booth and Company 1863–1958

A.H. JOHN

Routledge
Taylor & Francis Group

LONDON AND NEW YORK

First published in 1959

Published in 2006 by
Routledge
2 Park Square, Milton Park, Abingdon, Oxfordshire OX14 4RN
711 Third Avenue, New York, NY 10017

First issued in paperback 2014

Routledge is an imprint of the Taylor and Francis Group, an informa business

© 1959 Routledge

All rights reserved. No part of this book may be reprinted or reproduced or
utilized in any form or by any electronic, mechanical, or other means, now
known or hereafter invented, including photocopying and recording, or in
any information storage or retrieval system, without permission in writing
from the publishers.

The publishers have made every effort to contact authors and copyright
holders of the works reprinted in the *Economic History* series. This has not
been possible in every case, however, and we would welcome
correspondence from those individuals or organisations we have been
unable to trace.

These reprints are taken from original copies of each book. In many cases
the condition of these originals is not perfect. The publisher has gone to
great lengths to ensure the quality of these reprints, but wishes to point out
that certain characteristics of the original copies will, of necessity, be
apparent in reprints thereof.

British Library Cataloguing in Publication Data
A CIP catalogue record for this book
is available from the British Library

A Liverpool Merchant House
ISBN 0-415-38159-2 (volume)
ISBN 0-415-37796-X (subset)
ISBN 0-415-28619-0 (set)

ISBN13: 978-1-138-86512-9 (pbk)
ISBN13: 978-0-415-38159-8 (hbk)

Routledge Library Editions: Economic History

A LIVERPOOL MERCHANT HOUSE

A LIVERPOOL
MERCHANT HOUSE

BEING THE HISTORY OF

Alfred Booth and Company

1863-1958

BY A. H. JOHN

Reader in Economic History
University of London

Ruskin House

GEORGE ALLEN & UNWIN LTD

MUSEUM STREET LONDON

First published in Great Britain 1959

This book is copyright under the Berne Convention. Apart from any fair dealing for the purpose of private study, research, criticism, or review, as permitted under the Copyright Act, 1956, no portion may be reproduced by any process without written permission. Enquiry should be made to the publisher.

© *George Allen & Unwin Ltd., 1959*

PREFACE

This is an account of a family business, written primarily for those who are, or have been, associated with it; but written also in the hope that it may be found of some value by those who are interested in the history of English economic development during the past century. There may also be something for future students of this eventful hundred years. The subject, which in itself is of importance, has two other attractions. It represents a further chapter in the story of that remarkable group of Unitarian families who played so conspicuous a part in the social and economic life of nineteenth century Liverpool : and it reflects the business career of one of their most outstanding personalities, the Rt. Hon. Charles Booth, P.C., F.R.S.

In writing what is virtually a family history it is impossible to avoid being biographical, but I have also attempted to analyze the problems with which successive generations of partners have been faced and to set them in their economic context. As in the case of many other firms, war took its toll of the earlier records, especially on the shipping side of the business; but the partnership letters have survived intact and are the main source of the information contained within these pages. I have been able to consult various members of the company, and I am grateful for the freedom allowed me to make my own judgments. I should perhaps add that, to avoid a lavish use of footnotes, quotations from the partnership letters have not been given a precise reference, although this has naturally been done with regard to material used from other sources.

I am indebted to Mr George Booth, then chairman of Alfred Booth and Company, for the opportunity of writing this book; to his successor, Mr J. W. Booth, and to Mr Edmund Booth, chairman of the Unit Construction Company, for their encouragement. I have learned a great deal from Mr O. S. Penton, Mr T. J. Randolph, Mr F. G. Heise, Mr Charles Good, and Mr E. B. Deyes; and I owe much to Mr S. Whinyates, secretary of the Booth Steamship Company, as well as to his colleagues, for their ever-ready help. I thank them all. My greatest debt, however, is to Mr Daniel Booth both for his critical comments and for his friendly, patient explaining.

A. H. JOHN

CONTENTS

ILLUSTRATIONS

after page 128

AN ABRIDGED GENEALOGICAL TABLE OF THE BOOTH, FLETCHER AND CROMPTON FAMILIES

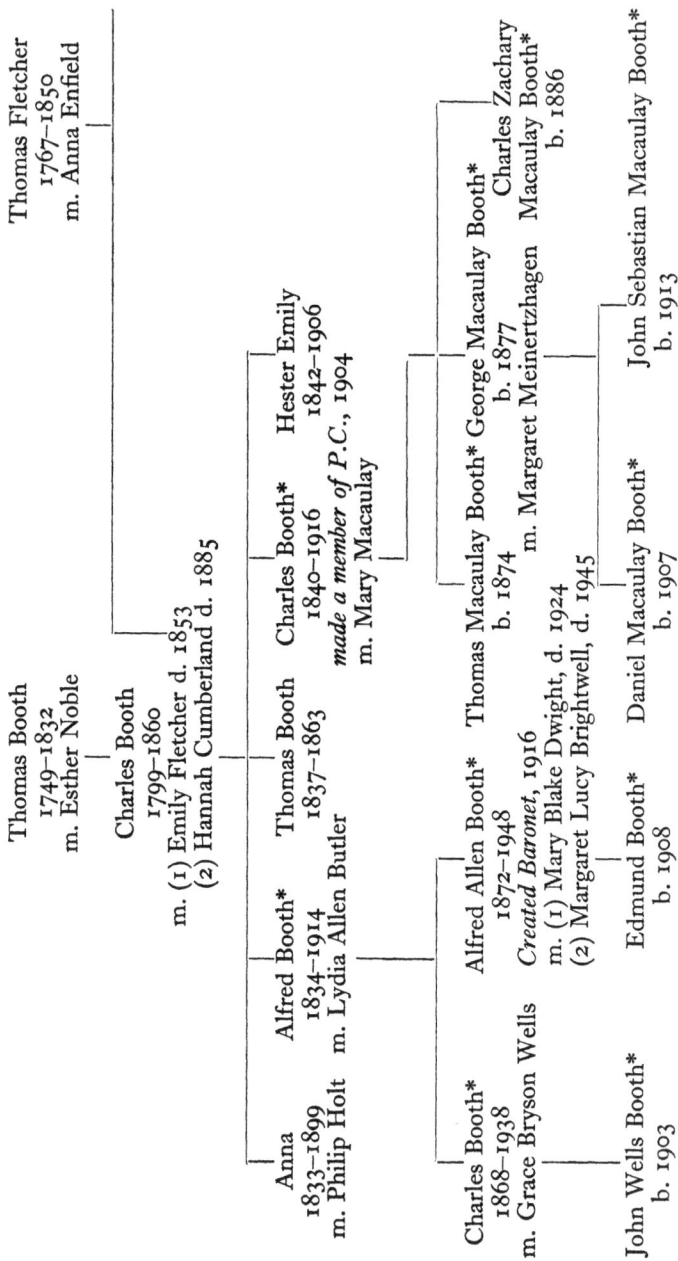

Thomas Booth
1749–1832
m. Esther Noble

Thomas Fletcher
1767–1850
m. Anna Enfield

Charles Booth
1799–1860
m. (1) Emily Fletcher d. 1853
(2) Hannah Cumberland d. 1885

Anna
1833–1899
m. Philip Holt

Alfred Booth*
1834–1914
m. Lydia Allen Butler

Thomas Booth
1837–1863

Charles Booth*
1840–1916
made a member of P.C., 1904
m. Mary Macaulay

Hester Emily
1842–1906

Charles Booth*
1868–1938
m. Grace Bryson Wells

Alfred Allen Booth*
1872–1948
Created Baronet, 1916
m. (1) Mary Blake Dwight, d. 1924
(2) Margaret Lucy Brightwell, d. 1945

Thomas Macaulay Booth*
b. 1874

George Macaulay Booth*
b. 1877
m. Margaret Meinertzhagen

Charles Zachary
Macaulay Booth*
b. 1886

John Wells Booth*
b. 1903

Edmund Booth*
b. 1908

Daniel Macaulay Booth*
b. 1907

John Sebastian Macaulay Booth*
b. 1913

*members of the firm of Alfred Booth & Company

AN ABRIDGED GENEALOGICAL TABLE OF THE BOOTH, FLETCHER AND CROMPTON FAMILIES

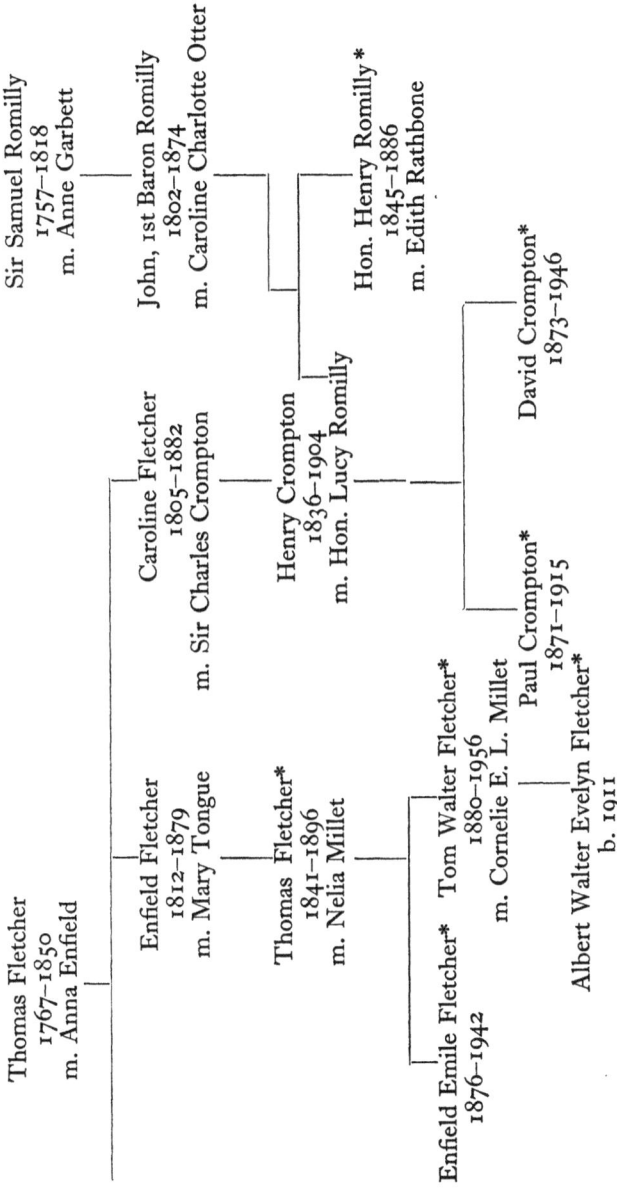

Thomas Fletcher
1767–1850
m. Anna Enfield

Sir Samuel Romilly
1757–1818
m. Anne Garbett

Enfield Fletcher
1812–1879
m. Mary Tongue

Caroline Fletcher
1805–1882
m. Sir Charles Crompton

John, 1st Baron Romilly
1802–1874
m. Caroline Charlotte Otter

Thomas Fletcher*
1841–1896
m. Nelia Millet

Henry Crompton
1836–1904
m. Hon. Lucy Romilly

Hon. Henry Romilly*
1845–1886
m. Edith Rathbone

Tom Walter Fletcher*
1880–1956
m. Cornelie E. L. Millet

Paul Crompton*
1871–1915

David Crompton*
1873–1946

Enfield Emile Fletcher*
1876–1942

Albert Walter Evelyn Fletcher*
b. 1911

CHAPTER 1

The Booth Family

The story of Messrs. Alfred Booth and Company is, in its origins and for most of its subsequent existence, part of the history of Liverpool. Two generations of the family had already been notable figures in the economic and social life of the port when Alfred and Charles Booth founded their partnership in 1863; and almost a century had passed since the first Booths left the surrounding countryside to seek careers in this rising centre of trade. Liverpool was then a town of some 30,000 inhabitants divided into four newly created parishes. Its growing wealth was to be seen in the handsome, solidly built houses of its merchants, in a school and infirmary supported by public subscriptions, and in an elegant, if largely unused, Exchange. All this was the outward expression of the town's increasing participation in the profitable Colonial trade; for, looking towards the Atlantic from the mouth of a wide, but dangerous, estuary, it was inevitable that its future should be in the commerce between the countries whose shores bordered that ocean. In the middle of the 18th century 'the older concern with the Greenland fisheries and the salt trade was still strong; shipbuilding, the Virginian tobacco and the wine trades were well begun, the heyday of sugar and slavery was yet to be'.[1] Liverpool merchants represented a quarter of the membership of the Royal African Company, and their interests in the West Indies and America were already considerable. By this date, the tonnage of shipping annually entering and leaving the river had increased fourfold since 1700: and, while these vessels had then been loaded, either on the strands near the town or while riding afloat on the Cheshire side of

---

[1] S. G. Checkland, 'Economic Attitudes in Liverpool, 1793-1807.' *The Economic History Review*, 2nd Series, Vol. 5, No. 1, 1952, p. 58.

the river, they were now accommodated in two docks. But substantial as had been the growth of Liverpool in this first half-century, its spectacular expansion came with the later development of the port's hinterland. From 1760 onwards, pottery, metals and hardware from the Midlands, salt from Cheshire and, above all, textile goods of all kinds, moved in increasing quantities, by river and canal navigation, to the port. Outward cargoes were balanced by an inward traffic in raw cotton, timber and grain, swelling the existing trade in colonial produce. Upon this growth, the changed status of America after 1783 had no permanent ill-effects. By 1800, the port could boast of five docks and a further fourfold increase in shipping; representing about a sixth of all the tonnage cleared from British ports, in contrast to a twenty-fourth in 1716. By 1850, the volume of shipping leaving the port had again multiplied twelvefold since the beginning of the century, and the value of the inward cargoes had reached over £31 million. In their rate of growth, Liverpool and Manchester were the outstanding expressions of the industrialism 'which had been coming over England like a climatic change'.

Thomas Booth, the grandfather of Alfred and Charles Booth, arrived in Liverpool in 1767, when the tide of this expansion was running strongly. He was 'the younger son of a yeoman farmer and small landowner in Orford', near Warrington, where the family had been established since at least the sixteenth century. In company with his brother, George, Thomas Booth was apprenticed to a corn merchant, by the name of Dodson, then living in Clayton Square. On the expiration of their articles, possibly in 1774, the brothers established themselves as corn factors at 17, King Street, Liverpool; just over a decade before John Gladstone, the founder of another famous Liverpool family, left Leith and established the firm of Corrie, Gladstone and Bradshaw in the same trade. 'The two men were very dissimilar in character', wrote Thomas Booth's eldest son. 'My Uncle George was grave and thoughtful, slow in coming to a decision, fond of intricate calculations, whether in matters of account or of mechanical problems. My father was a man of business prompt, energetic and decisive. They were many years in partnership and it will be readily understood that my father took the lead as acting partner, while my uncle generally acquiesced in his proceedings'.[2]

That the partnership prospered is evident. The brothers were men of character and acumen, and business conditions were in their favour. Under the pressure of a growing population finding increasing employment in manufacture, England had ceased on balance to be an exporter of grain in the middle 'sixties of the 18th century, and within two decades had become a permanent importer. Much of this grain came from Ireland and north Germany, for which trade Liverpool merchants were excellently placed, having a rapidly expanding market in the hinterland of the port. By 1789, fifteen years after beginning an independent business, Thomas and George Booth were sufficiently well established for Thomas to correspond with Lord Hawkesbury, President of the Board of Trade, on matters relating to the corn laws. As was commonly the case with prosperous merchants of the eighteenth and early nineteenth centuries, they were owners, or part-owners, of several ships, which they employed in the carriage of grain both coastwise and from overseas. The largest ship of their small fleet was the *Esther*, which according to a Lloyd's description in 1798, was a vessel of 210 tons, carrying six guns and noted as a regular trader to the Baltic.

Recognition as spokesmen for the grain trade was but the beginning of a long activity in the town's economic, social and political life. The brothers were, for example, among the founders and directors of the St George Fire Office, opened in 1801, with a capital of £300,000, for the insuring of houses, warehouses, ships and cargoes in docks and harbours. The venture had, however, a short history, for the heavy losses occasioned by the burning of the Goree Warehouses led in 1803 to its amalgamation with the Imperial Fire Insurance Company, another Liverpool concern in which the family maintained an active interest. Thomas and George Booth were, too, among the earliest members of the Athenaeum News Room and served on a succession of local committees from the one established to erect a memorial to Nelson in 1808, to that elected in 1822 to present a 'public address to Mr Joseph Hume

[2] H. A. Whitting, *Alfred Booth; Memories and Letters*, pp. 7-8.

B

for his services on the subject of Economy and Retrenchment in public expenditure'.

However prominent later members of the family were in the cause of free trade, the first generation were typical eighteenth century merchants in their attitude towards trade regulation. This is evident from the letters of Thomas Booth to Lord Hawkesbury. Trade and shipping, he argued, could best be carried on within the framework of beneficent legislation; and he objected strongly, but unsuccessfully, to the import of grain in foreign vessels during the near famine years of 1799-1800. These sentiments were made public in a pamphlet written by his brother entitled *Observations on lowering the Rent of Land and on the Corn Laws*, published in 1814. Here George Booth attacked the view that high rents had any appreciable effect on the price of grain and advocated complete protection for agriculture, looking to improved techniques to produce the corn necessary for an increasing population. The pamphlet was reprinted in 1815, when he published '*Observations on Paper Currency, the Bank of England Notes, and on the Principles of Coinage, and a metallic circulating Medium*'. In company with many provincial and metropolitan merchants he maintained that the issue of paper money had not caused the war-time rise in prices, and thus had no effect on the depreciated state of the pound sterling. This he based upon the somewhat dubious argument that a fall in the value of money must affect all commodities equally: but the price of certain goods, such as coal, had not risen since 1806: therefore the upward movement of prices must have been due to other causes. Of these the high level of taxation and the size of the National Debt were of foremost importance. Like many other members of the Unitarian group in Liverpool, he regarded the 'invention of the funding system' as 'one of the greatest curses that ever afflicted mankind'. Characteristically, he blamed 'speculative politicians with all their professed contempt for the opinions of practical men'.

George Booth remained unmarried and died shortly before his brother, whose death occurred in 1832. The latter, after leaving King Street, first settled in Rodney Street, and finally built himself a house, called The Lodge, in Toxeth Park, that part of the town favoured by the leading Nonconformist merchants of his day. By his marriage with Miss Esther Noble, of Lancaster, Thomas Booth had five sons and four daughters. Like their uncle, his daughters remained unmarried: and his second son, George, died early in life. Of the other sons, Henry Booth, the eldest, became a well-known figure, not only in Liverpool, but in the English railway world of the middle decades of the nineteenth century. He was one of the founders of the famous Liverpool and Manchester Railway Company, of which he was for many years a director and its secretary. Henry Booth wrote much on free trade, on social problems generally and on railway questions. He was a man of considerable mechanical skill, to whose credit can be placed several important inventions in railway engineering, the best known of which was the multi-tubular boiler, first used in the *Rocket* at the Rainhill trials of 1829. The second son, James Booth, C.B., after being at St John's College, Cambridge (despite his Unitarian upbringing), became successively Counsel to the Speaker and Secretary of the Board of Trade. As a young barrister, he served on the Royal Commission on Municipal Corporations in 1833: and in his retirement was a member of that which investigated trade unions in 1867. The family business in the grain trade was carried on by the younger sons, Thomas and Charles Booth.

In 1829, Charles Booth married Emily Fletcher, a daughter of Thomas Fletcher, a West Indian merchant and later an unsuccessful banker. They had five children: Anna, who became the wife of Philip Holt, a founder of the Ocean Steamship Company; Alfred and Charles, the creators of Alfred Booth and Company; and Thomas and Emily Booth. This union of members of two of the leading Nonconformist families was characteristic of the religious and social background of early nineteenth century Liverpool. For its society in this period divided itself fairly clearly into two broad groups: the whig, Anglican families typified by the Gladstones, and the more radical, dissenting group, amongst whom the Unitarians were predominant. Formerly members of the old Presbyterian Church, the Booths, like others of this persuasion, moved into Unitarianism at the end of the eighteenth century. Thomas and George Booth were founder-members of, and prominent office-holders in, the

Renshaw Street Chapel, built in 1811 as an offshoot of the older assembly at Benn's Garden. 'Architecturally the Chapel may be described as the spirit of Puritanism turned into stone, a fortress built foursquare against the assaults of Satan, an Ironside among chapels, with no beauty that men should desire it, save that of fitness for its purpose. This was defined by the Open Trust Deed as the worship of God, whose Divine Nature, as indicated by the architecture, was clearly that of *Ein feste Burg*.'[3] Here at Benn's Garden, at 'Key Street, Paradise Street, and at Gateacre Chapel, at the turn of the century foregathered families even then of note, and later to be of great influence.'[4] Later in the century, when a grandson of Thomas Booth was a prominent member of the Chapel, the character of its congregation had changed but little. 'Walking down Renshaw Street about noon on a Sunday morning in the eighties you would have passed a long line of carriage-and-pairs . . . awaiting the exit from the Chapel of Rathbones, Holts, Jevons, Gaskells, Brunners, Tates, Jones, Thornleys, Mellys, Hollands and Gairs, their stately locomotion to and from Chapel on a Sunday morning being then one of the sights of Liverpool.'[5] The collective influence of these families on the trade of Liverpool was paralleled only by that in Birmingham of such 'high powered and strongly individualized' industrialists as the Chamberlains, the Kenricks, the Nettlefolds and others who made up the congregation of the Unitarian Church of the Messiah.

These Liverpool Unitarian families comprised the society in which the Booths moved; a society which was the more closely knit by the fact of intermarriage. The Thornleys and the Fletchers were cousins of the third generation of Booths, so also were the children of Mr Justice Crompton and those of Sir Henry Roscoe: while through the marriage of Anna Booth to Philip Holt the ramifications of these alliances was extended still further. Unorthodox in theology but uncompromising in the practice of Nonconformist ethics, cultured, and radical in political outlook—it was from this group of families that many

[3] L. P. Jacks, *The Confessions of an Octogenarian*, p. 138.
[4] S. G. Checkland, *op. cit.*, p. 63.
[5] L. P. Jacks, *op. cit.*, p. 141 *et seq.*

who later were to be so influential originated. They represent one of the great family clans which formed the basic structure of contemporary middle class society both in the intellectual and the business world. It was in the offices of such Nonconformist merchants that successive generations of the Booths were trained; and later, it was from the resources of this same group that much of Alfred Booth and Company's capital was obtained. Neither the beginnings of the firm nor the social work of the Booth family can be fully understood except in its Nonconformist background.

Alfred, born in 1834, and Charles, born in 1840, spent the greater part of their earlier years in an attractive Regency-style house built by their father in Croxteth Lane, facing the newly laid-out Prince's Park. Alfred was educated first at the Liverpool Mechanics Institute and then at the Edgebaston Proprietary School; Charles Booth, with his elder brother, Thomas, at the Royal Institution School, Liverpool. Their upbringing was typically that of a prosperous middle class family of the time. The more serious matters of school and chapel were lightened by visits to concerts and operas in Liverpool, by journeys to relations and friends, by 'joint expeditions undertaken in holiday time, in company with the seven Cromptons, the two Roscoes, and above all, with Thomas and Henrietta Fletcher',[6] the children of their uncle, Enfield Fletcher. Like their father and grandfather, the young Booths took an active share in the affairs of the Renshaw Street Chapel. Their names appear in its contemporary records and many of their father's surviving letters are given over to news of its activities. 'Over at Dukenfield yesterday,' it was written in June, 1858, 'as a delegate from our congregation to the 209th anniversary of the Lancashire and Cheshire Presbyterian Association. The chapel was handsome but decorated with flowers which was nice but Puseyistic.' The youthful Charles Booth, on the other hand, had, so he informed his brother, 'been doing the quarterly characters of my Sunday School boys this week . . . Bell, of course, had a capital character. He has not been late or absent once in the whole quarter and his mother seemed very much pleased. Osman is, I think, my worst boy, but I dare say I shall

[6] M. C. Booth, *Charles Booth; A Memoir*, p. 4.

get over him in time, and he had rather a bad character. However, his mother promised to see that he learned his hymns and brought his book for the future. I manage the class very easily when there are not more than 6 or 7, but when it comes to 9 or 10, it becomes very difficult to keep them quiet. I think it is too many in one class, but I suppose if I lose any it will be my best ones.' In this and in the work among the poor of Liverpool undertaken by the Unitarian chapels, lay the origin of what later was to be the enquiry into London life and labour.

In 1850 Alfred Booth was apprenticed to Lamport and Holt, a well-known Liverpool merchant house, one of whose senior partners—Mr Lamport—was his father's second cousin. His brother, Thomas, went on to Trinity College, Cambridge (again despite his Unitarian background); and afterwards served his articles as a solicitor, but died in Constantinople in 1863 before beginning his career. Charles Booth, the youngest son, followed his brother into Lamport and Holt, where his father reported that he had 'taken to office work uncommonly well and is in favour with Mr Lamport', known to the brothers as the 'Lamb'. Such a training in a merchant house of this type would normally have involved some experience in the management of shipping; and at this time, when steam was slowly gaining a hold upon sea transport, this aspect of their apprenticeship was both valuable and opportune. For 'Lamport and Holt had been interested, among other things, in sending sailing ships to the Mediterranean to take part in the Alexandria trade. In conjunction with James Moss and Company they were beginning, in the early 1850's to replace sailing ships by small steamships.'[7] The knowledge thus gained was to be of the greatest significance in the subsequent careers of the two brothers.

The placing of Alfred and Charles Booth in Lamport and Holt marked the end of the family business in the grain trade. Like many farmers, it is not improbable that the smaller grain merchants suffered considerably from the depression caused by the long fall in prices after the Napoleonic War. The ownership of sailing vessels was certainly given up by Thomas and the elder Charles Booth in this period; and it is possible that other aspects of the business were abandoned when they retired. The

[7] F. E. Hyde, *Blue Funnel*, p. 11.

death of Charles Booth in 1860 thus closed an era in the business history of the family; and his sons, when their apprenticeships were over, were under the necessity of finding new spheres of activity.

CHAPTER II

Years of War: Years of Experience

1857-1865

In 1857 Alfred Booth, then twenty-three years of age, completed his apprenticeship with Lamport and Holt; and to gain further experience, sailed almost immediately to take up a temporary post in the New York office of Rathbone and Company, one of the greatest of Liverpool merchant houses, with interests in Shanghai, Canton and London. Henry Gair and William Lidderdale, the two managers of the American branch, were already well known to the Booth family both as businessmen and as prominent members of the Renshaw Street Chapel. Lidderdale was afterwards to become Governor of the Bank of England and the pilot who steered the City through the Baring crisis of 1890. Alfred Booth's arrival in New York coincided with the financial troubles of 1857, and under the guidance of these two shrewd men he learned much that was later to prove of great value.

That Alfred Booth as a young Liverpool man should have found opportunities of employment in the United States so quickly is not surprising. The ties between Liverpool and New York were as close as those between Liverpool and London. As it has been said 'the United States and Great Britain stood in closer relations to each other than the normal definition of "international trade" '; as a consequence, 'it is more useful to think in terms of a single, Atlantic economy, directed towards the exploitation of American resources for mutual profit, than of two more independent, and competitive economies. Until at least 1850 America grew economically under the guidance of an informal partnership between, on the one hand, Liverpool shippers and emigrant brokers, London merchant bankers,

British iron, hardware and textile manufacturers, and on the other, the merchants, bankers, and transport promoters of Boston, New York and Philadelphia and the cotton planters of the Deep South.[1] In these circumstances, his journey across the Atlantic was as natural as, given his background, it could possibly be.

During the two years of his appointment, Alfred Booth remained uncertain as to his future, although determined not to settle permanently in America. He refused an offer of a partnership with A. P. Thornley in a cotton broking business and finally agreed to spend a further year in New York with Rathbone and Company, at a salary of $1,500. 'It is particularly gratifying to me,' wrote his father, 'to see your services so highly valued.' It was during this proposed last year in America that the opportunity of forming an independent business seems to have presented itself. Deliberate consideration of these ideas was, however, prevented by the sudden and unexpected death of his father, Charles Booth, in February 1860, and a hurried decision was made largely to provide an opportunity for the younger brother. Accordingly, a partnership was almost immediately formed with an American, by the name of Walden, to establish a merchant house primarily for the importing of English light leather into the U.S.A. To these activities was added an agency for Alfred and Philip Holt, whose steamers traded between Liverpool, the West Indies and New York. An office and showrooms were obtained in 57, Broad Street, away from that part of New York inhabited by the leather industries, but sufficiently near the docks to facilitate the other work of the business.

What led to the choice of this particular trade is a matter of conjecture, but certain considerations are clear. The great staple trades of Liverpool were already dominated by well-established firms, some of them of great wealth. Cotton, for example, was imported on consignment by merchants, who, for a commission shared with the selling broker, were responsible for its disposal in England. The large trade in tinplate lay in the hands of the important American house, Phelps, Dodge

---

[1] Frank Thistlethwaite, 'Commercial America' in *British Essays on American History*, edited by H. C. Allen and C. P. Hill, p. 103.

and Company, who 'had it their own way, dealing direct with the manufacturers for cash and controlling them by advances'. The place of the newcomer of limited means was thus either in the less profitable branches of commerce, or in the smaller trades where profit represented the earnings of specialized knowledge. On the other hand, the economic expansion of America, gathering pace under the impetus of a rapidly growing population, created demands for raw materials which could not entirely, and in some cases not even partially, be supplied from home sources. It was in these relatively new and expanding trades that the small merchant, willing to acquire specialized knowledge, might find an opening. The import of light leathers, made from sheep and goat skins, was one such trade. The raw material thus provided went to the tanners, leather dressers, and to the manufacturers of footwear, gloves, hats and bookbindings; most of whom, at this time, were located in the eastern states. Gloversville in Fulton County, some one hundred and sixty miles north of New York, was an important centre of glovemaking; while Massachusetts held the greatest number of boot and shoe factories, with Boston as their largest single location. In New York itself, there existed a wide range of leather industries, particularly in the area known as the 'Swamp'. It might well have been, therefore, that Walden was already concerned in some way with the leather trade and had met Alfred Booth in the course of business with Rathbone and Company. At all events, here was an opportunity for the young Englishman to establish his own business which, with an American partner, would enable him to return home to manage the Liverpool house. At the same time it made provision for his younger brother, Charles.

The beginnings of the venture were inauspicious enough. The outbreak of the Civil War followed the signing of the partnership deed by only a few months, adding further problems to the many which normally beset a new concern. Unlike the majority of Liverpool merchants, Alfred and Charles Booth sympathized with the Northern rather than with the Southern States. When the Confederate Loan was issued in 1863, Alfred wrote that it had been taken up in Paris, Amsterlam, Frankfurt, London and Liverpool, 'so England will not have to bear the whole odium of it', and added, with approval, a comment of William Rathbone—a kindred spirit in this matter—that the loan was 'a disgrace to this country'. But with the initial problems of Walden and Booth and the dislocations of war came additional trouble. Walden developed signs of insanity and was, by January 1863, permanently confined to a mental home. The immediate responsibility for dealing with this crisis fell to the youthful Charles Booth, who had gone to America in the early stages of Walden's illness; his elder brother being in Liverpool for the purpose of dealing with matters arising from the deaths of their father and brother, Thomas, and to open a Liverpool office at 5, India Buildings. Early in 1863, therefore, the partnership with Walden was formally dissolved, and the firms of Alfred Booth and Company, Liverpool, and Booth and Company, New York, came into being, with the brothers as partners. 'What one feels about our business in New York,' wrote Alfred Booth when matters had been settled, 'is that constituted as it now is—you and I—it is rather placed there by force of circumstances than by choice of ours; and that if it were a fresh start, two situated as we are would hardly be expected to establish their business at New York. You, however, do not dislike the idea of remaining out for a while (the people here will be wanting you back badly soon, I know) and I have no objection to taking my turn, and I do not see what better can be done than carry on this business so far as I am concerned; but what you want, active, constant work and responsibility, might be found perhaps, without going so far for it.'

The new partnership made little immediate change in either the size or the security of their business. With a capital of about £14,000, largely made up of monies inherited from their father, and with credit facilities granted by such friends as Alfred and Philip Holt, Rathbone and Company and by Lamport and Holt, skins were purchased to the extent of some £2,500 a month. These were of two kinds: vegetable (sumac) tanned sheepskins, largely used for the upper parts of boots and shoes, and the split, untanned, skins preserved in pickle. These 'splits', produced by both tanners and fellmongers, consisted of the upper and stouter division of the skin, called the grain, and the under and thinner one, the flesh. As the former could take a high finish, it was used in the manufacture of gloves and handbags; while fleshes were employed in the making of japanned and imitation chamois leather. The leather was obtained from the Bermondsey tanners; the split skins from a number of Midland firms—the Turneys, newly established at Trent Bridge, Boots of Leicester, or from Johnstone at Bootle. The goods were warehoused in Liverpool and then shipped to New York. Without much expert knowledge each shipment involved some unsaleable stock, and in New York itself selling proved to be a much slower affair than was expected. Because of this, the brothers made strenuous efforts in these early years to expand their activities in other directions. £700 was invested in the Weed Sewing Machine Company, and Alfred Booth spent much fruitless time trying to sell its products in England. The import of American foodstuffs into this country during the bad harvests of 1859-62, tempted them into remitting a substantial part of their American receipts in the form of wheat and flour, lard and tallow, pork and bacon. These commodities were sold in Liverpool by a broker, generally for cash or on fourteen days' credit. Their most rewarding work, however, lay in the buying and selling orders which came their way because of the dislocation of normal trade channels during the American Civil War. Between 1864 and 1867 they bought regularly for such cotton brokers as G. and A. Shute, and James Howell, or for cotton spinners like the Hopwoods of Blackburn. But it was clear 'that if we are to get any orders it will not be from the big swells, and small people of a more likely kind is all we can expect.' Hence the financial standing of their clients was a question of importance. Where there were doubts, it was customary to attach the lading documents to the bill of exchange as a form of security; although such documentary bills were difficult to discount, especially with the notoriously strict Heywood's Bank. Sometimes such precautions proved unnecessary : 'Mr E. L. Jones,' wrote Charles Booth, 'is exceedingly wealthy (so) Mr Thompson told me with the most delicious banker's smile.'

Despite the rise in American commodity prices after 1861, the result of their first four years of business was merely to pay the interest on the capital employed. The sewing machine venture was recognized as a mistake and abandoned in 1864. The outcome of the trade in foodstuffs between 1862 and 1864 was a net loss of £185; £30,000 worth of sheepskins shipped in 1863-4 yielded a profit of only £140 and the 2½% commission earned by Booth and Company, New York. A further disappointment was the loss of the Holt steamship agency when the West Indian line was sold to the West Indian and Pacific Steamship Company in 1864. It was perhaps hardly to be expected that such widely dispersed activities could be successfully managed. The import of foodstuffs required great experience and substantial capital, neither of which was possessed by the two young men. Even in the export of skins there was still much to be learned before competence in the handling of the trade was attained. Vowing that he would never again buy a cask of grains, Charles Booth observed to his brother, 'I was never able to tell whether the skins were right or not and Turney could always shut me up.' It was a period of disillusionment and uncertainty, when the continuance of the leather business and of the New York house lay in the balance. 'Shall we go and try our fortunes at the Antipodes or join Robert Crompton in sheep-farming in La Plata?' suggested Alfred Booth light-heartedly; but with Charles, younger and more closely attached to the business world, the possibility of failure was more keenly felt. 'I thought we were swells and I find we were fools. I laughed at the idea that I should have to lose my money to gain experience, but so it has been.'

The troubles of these early years revealed clearly the remarkably complementary characters of the two brothers; reminiscent, in many ways, of the relationship existing between George and Thomas Booth half a century earlier. In their fine intelligence, their unremitting industry and their deep sense of social obligation, both were in the best tradition of Liverpool merchants of the nineteenth century. Yet to Alfred Booth a career in trade was the result of necessity rather than of choice. 'I wish it had been in your power to follow your bent and lead a country life,' wrote his father in 1859, 'and I hope you may never be so much engrossed in mercantile life as to be prevented from (enjoying) to some extent your natural tastes. I am inclined to think that had you taken to the life of an artist you would have succeeded far better than the average, but whether you would have risen to the top of the tree to which so few attain is of course doubtful.' And again, 'I think you are right in preferring a moderate income pleasantly earned to a large one attended with disagreeable circumstances.' To these sentiments Alfred Booth remained unswervingly faithful, and for their attainment served thirty years. With his brother it was otherwise. 'To him,' as his wife has written, 'the great forces that stir the pendulum of trade; the hazards to be incurred in new portions of the work of a great concern; the sharp reminder of failure given by the actual loss of money when undertaking had been begun too rashly, or conducted with insufficient insight; above all, the contact with a set of men working towards one end, and in hourly touch with the realities of existence; all this delighted and absorbed him.'[2]

To a man of Alfred Booth's inclinations, backed as they were by a deep reserve, the routine of business was a self-discipline, which as the years passed grew more irksome. 'You seem to look upon yourself as Mazeppa,' exclaimed his younger brother, 'and business as the horse.' He contemplated retiring in 1867 shortly after his marriage, again in 1877, and finally did so ten years later. He was a man of great integrity, insistent upon the observance of well-defined, even rigid, principles of business; kindly, but intolerant of stupidity. When, in 1882, it emerged that the firm's Brazilian agents had paid £1,000 to the President's agent for the Manáos-New York contract, his reaction was characteristic. 'It is certainly a degradation I never imagined being brought to and I cannot tell you how I desire we could be clear of the whole thing.' It required the combined efforts of his partners and of his friends, the Holts, to persuade him that the firm was powerless to cancel the contract at will. and that little practical good would result from the repudiation of their agent in what was the general method of conducting Brazilian affairs in the nineteenth century. The episode served, however, to strengthen his wish to retire and hastened the establishment of the company's own agency on the Amazon river. This dislike of commercial activity gave him

[2] M. C. Booth, *Charles Booth; A Memoir*, p. 94.

a certain detachment, which provided poise in adversity and a sound judgment of men and affairs. His main interest was the leather trade, and it was upon his knowledge of skins that this part of the partnership's activities was based. But the impress of his general attitude towards business has been enduring and unmistakeable in the conduct of Alfred Booth and Company.

Charles Booth's approach to business was wider and more theoretical. It rested upon a belief that industry and trade were both necessary and honourable, capable of being conducted in a 'civilized' and rational manner. Profits were the payment for services rendered to the community: not to be sought after greedily, but the just reward of efficiency: 'the inexorable court of personal profit and loss, to which every individual firm must submit, and by which it learns both prudence and wise daring.'[3] His technique in the conduct of affairs lay essentially in the analysis of broad trends, as shown by statistical evidence, and the creation of an organization by which the emerging pattern of wants could be met. The need for 'system' in business was, in his eyes, a dominant necessity. 'We must put an end to this sloppy brotherly way of doing business,' he wrote in 1866, 'or we shall pay dearly for it. The lazy impulse not to think how a thing will be, but to leave everything to the other won't do.' The structure of his mind made his judgment in immediate, day-to-day, problems less ready than that of either his brother or their partner and cousin, Thomas Fletcher. 'But I want your real opinion on these matters, you have a better judgment than I have'—is a constant expression in his letters to his brother. Determined 'to break down this stupid "Booth reserve" in myself and in others so far as I can,' he aroused great loyalty and affection among those with whom he worked. Tenacious of purpose, he was capable of labouring slowly and steadily for the fulfilment of plans, themselves the product of long and careful thought. The secret of the eventful success of the business lay in the interaction of Charles Booth's long-term considerations with the sound practical judgments of his partners. If the tactics were theirs, the strategy was his.

Such being the character of Charles Booth, it is not surprising that his early experience of Anglo-American trade should

[3] M. C. Booth, *op. cit.*, pp. 94-95.

have led him to consider an alternative field of activity. Back in England in early 1864, he found increasing attention being paid to steam navigation, especially by his Liverpool contemporaries. There were already regular steam services to the Dutch, Belgian, French and Mediterranean ports; the transatlantic service of the Cunard Company was reputed to be paying a third of the Liverpool port dues; while the Holts, together with the London-based Royal Mail Line, had already pioneered the West Indian route. And now, in the early 'sixties, two companies were in process of being established for the Canadian trade, the National Steam Navigation Company was being floated to provide a service between Liverpool and the southern states of America, and Lamport and Holt were on the point of inaugurating their South Brazilian line. With his closest associates, Alfred and Philip Holt, the topic of conversation 'morning, noon and night' concerned the possibilities of steam-driven vessels. Alfred Holt, already far advanced with his experiments in high-pressure engines, was engaged, with his brother, Philip, in making ambitious plans. Encouraged by the Holts, Charles Booth also embarked upon a 'scheme'. 'If this experiment of theirs answers,' he wrote to his brother, 'we must all go in for it with all the money we can spare, and this adds another chance to the probability of our future being connected with steam. I think this is the large scheme towards which we ought to work, and I would let everything else suffer first. The real plan of succeeding in business is to choose such a course that the tide of affairs is with you—it is that more than individual talent that does it. Then average ability is all you need. Leave steamers as they are and they will get into any of the New York trades in which we are well placed. With the present protective tariffs on iron and foreign-built ships no American vessels can interfere with us and the plan of working steam trades with two centres is very sound and sure to be worked. With steam as it is it would come slowly. But if A.H. succeeds and the consumption of coal is reduced $\frac{1}{2}$, a complete revolution will follow and every sailing vessel will in time be driven out.'

These ideas were sound, even if another fifty years were to elapse before sailing ships were completely outmoded. For although the gross tonnage of steam-shipping increased from 275,000 tons in 1855 to 454,000 tons in 1860, and doubled again in the next five years, it still represented only a quarter of the total tonnage registered in this country. Since 1819 steam had made rapid progress in the coastwise trade, and after 1837, with the aid of heavy government subsidies, in the fast packet services for the carriage of mails. But in 1865 the steamship had not even touched the fringe of the business engaged in the carriage of bulky cargoes. In these early vessels, 'the volume of freight-earning space' was 'sacrificed to engine and boiler, and above all, the further capacity sacrificed to the stowage of coal, which on any but the shortest voyages practically monopolized the ship's carrying power.'[4] The consumption of coal alone was thirty tons a day in ships, which, in the main, were still paddle boats assisted by sail; screw propulsion gaining favour only after the middle of the century. The significance of Alfred Holt's experiments lay in the use of steam power on the long voyage by the more economical use of coal.

The results of this technical advance were posed in a letter from Charles to Alfred Booth early in 1864. 'You will perceive that the thing to be considered is what shape will steam trade eventually take—will it be established lines?—or free steamers going anywhere on charter like (sailing) ships?' The possibility of the dual function of liner and tramp steamer seems not to have been envisaged and was to be a later development. Steamships had been employed hitherto in the trade between stated ports, maintaining a specified arrival and departure date as far as the uncertain performance of their engines would permit; and the new compound engine made possible, in the first instance, the long voyage, rather than the profitable carriage of cheap bulky cargo. Hence, the answer to the question was the establishment of a regular voyage run on liner principles. This decided, the search for a route went on energetically throughout the latter part of 1864, against the background of disappointing American trade. A proposal for a New York-West Indian service was abandoned because of possible difficulties with an American crew: a New York-Newfoundland-Liverpool route was considered and rejected, as was a New York-Rio de

---

[4] R. H. Thornton, *British Shipping*, p. 15.

C

Janeiro scheme. Eventually it was decided that a plan of sail-ings based on Liverpool had a double advantage; Charles Booth would have the advice and practical assistance of the Holts, and money would be more easily raised for a venture based on a home port than for one centred abroad. The Holts were plan-ning to enter the China trade, and Charles Booth desired to establish a service to Calcutta, which represented an 'almost untouched trade of unlimited extent'. The difficulty here, how-ever, was the amount of capital required to make full use of the initial advantages. To begin with two boats was merely to create an opportunity for others, and to build a bigger fleet by means of a joint-stock company was too large an undertaking for two, as yet, unknown young men.

With Lamport and Holt already established in the trade to Rio de Janeiro and Pernambuco, it was finally agreed to enter that between Liverpool and the three northern ports of Brazil, then called Ceará, Maranham and Pará.[5] It was from Maranham that Brazilian cotton was first brought to England in 1781, and although the trade had grown in the succeeding seventy years, only thirty-nine ships cleared for these ports in 1851. The re-turn cargoes in 1856 consisted of cotton, sugar and coffee, and employed a mere 14/20,000 tons of shipping. It was thus one of the smallest of Liverpool trades, but one in which, it was thought, two steamships could establish a regular and re-munerative service. The one major difficulty was that, while the Maranham trade was open, that to Ceará and Pará was already in the hands of wealthy Liverpool merchant houses, from whose sailing ships powerful opposition could be ex-pected.

By January 1865, the initial trials of Alfred Holt's new engine in the *Cleator* had proved successful. 'It is wonderful to me,' wrote Charles Booth, 'that these engines have not been sooner arrived at, as every single part has been adopted separately ex-cept the high pressure itself.' But this had in fact occurred. 'In 1856 the Pacific Steam Navigation Company had added to their fleet two new ships, the *Inca* and *Valparaiso*, fitted with a com-pound engine designed by Elder and Randolph'; and 'if the im-plications of the new engine were not at once obvious, the ex-

[5] Now Fortaleza, Sâo Luiz and Belem respectively.

planation was no doubt partly to be found in the fact that the ships of the Pacific Steam Navigation Company were employed away from home.'[6] Alfred Holt's version of these engines, independently arrived at, however, proved to be more economical than those of Elder and Randolph. 'On the strength of the experience gained from the *Cleator*'s voyages, therefore, Alfred and Philip Holt laid down at a cost of £156,000, the *Agammemnon*, the *Ajax*, and the *Achilles*, each ship having a single crank compound tandem engine with the latest design of hull. With this working capital the Ocean Steamship Company was created. The Company was registered on January 1, 1865, and Alfred Holt issued the first circular to the public on January 16, 1866. It started to operate on July 1st of that year. Before this later date, however, on April 19th the *Agammemnon* with Captain Middleton in command, had sailed for China and the great adventure had begun.'[7]

While this enterprise was being established in No. 1 India Buildings, the Booths were planning their's in No. 5. In the early months of 1865 Charles Booth, with the help of the two Holt brothers, worked out the specifications of the proposed ships and set about raising the necessary additional capital. Here, unlike the Holt venture, the plan adopted was the traditional one. The value of the ships was divided into sixty-four parts and Alfred Booth and Company, as the managing owners, took up as many as its resources would allow. But like the Holts' company, the remainder was largely subscribed by friends and relatives, although not without some refusals. 'Uncle Booth was too old' to invest, John Crompton was cautious, William Holt promised but later withdrew, Currie and Avison were themselves building. Nevertheless the money was found within a month from, among others, William and Alfred Thornley, Edward Enfield, Captain Eills and Charles Booth's friends the Pranges.

Until the formation of the first Booth Steamship Company in 1881, the shipping side of the business continued to be organized in this way. Each vessel represented an individual partnership, with Alfred Booth and Company a common par-

[6] R. H. Thornton, *British Shipping*, p. 65.
[7] F. E. Hyde, *Blue Funnel*, p. 19.

ticipant in all. A separate account was opened for each round voyage and a profit or loss declared. From December 1868 until 1874 each voyage was charged £25 for 'Liverpool Management', a sum subsequently increased to £50 in 1874 and £58 in 1878. How often the profits were divided among the owners is not known, but it is clear that before so doing a deduction was made for the depreciation of the ships and for some form of reserve.

The year in which the shipping business was being planned also proved to be a more profitable one in the Booths' American trade. There was a steady flow of commissions which, by December 1865, showed a net profit of £600: and as the front rooms of the New York office had been let, expenses were substantially less. Uncertainty about the sheep-skin business thus began to recede, especially as Alfred Booth was anxious to continue the work so laboriously begun. In Liverpool, the Holts had given the partnership the North European forwarding agency for their new line to China, which, although small, was an additional source of income. Experience had shown, however, that operating an export business on their own account required far greater capital than they possessed, and far more than they would have when their share in the proposed two ships had been paid for. It was thus agreed to encourage tanners and fellmongers to consign their skins to America, and by so doing enable a larger business to be conducted on a given amount of capital. Two firms already employed Alfred Booth and Company for this purpose, and in February 1865, a third, E. J. Turney, of Nottingham, perhaps their most important client, agreed to do so. This tanning concern, although fairly recently established, had built up a large business on the Continent, and now wished to extend their markets in America, particularly for those types of sheepskin which could not be sold elsewhere. Alfred Booth and Company contracted to advance five-sixths of the cost of the invoice value, by the acceptance of a three or four months bill of exchange, and to charge a commission of 5% in addition to the costs involved in transport.

'It may be considered fixed, I think, that we go heart and soul into this steamer plan . . . and also that we keep on New

York.' In this way the lines upon which the future of the business were to develop were now established: an export of sheepskins, tanned and untanned, to the United States of America, and the provision of a steamship service to the North Brazilian ports. Thus the general policy of a 'widespread but generally inter-connected business, which provides a well balanced structure' came into being. Leather and shipping remained for long the two integrated and mutually supporting aspects of the firm's activities: just as leather and building are today. And it was in the success achieved in balancing the first group of these diverse trades that the unique contribution of Charles Booth was made to the growth of the concern.

CHAPTER III

The Sheepskin Trade
1865-1890

When the contracts were placed for the first two ships in February 1865, Alfred Booth was thirty and Charles Booth almost twenty-five years of age . The year had a double significance in the history of the firm: it witnessed the beginning of the venture into steam shipping and also the establishment of a commission house, thus marking the end of a period of probation in the business world. For the commission merchant, or factor, was, at the middle of the century, the most important figure in the organization of foreign trade in both this country and the United States. He might be a member of a general commission house like that of Baring Brothers or Rathbone Brothers, with branches in many parts of the world; or of a firm trading to one market, or in a single commodity. Such houses were not precluded from purchasing goods outright when occasion demanded, but they were principally the recognized agencies through which English manufacturers distributed their goods overseas. In the eighteen sixties, they were at the height of their importance, and later decades were to see a decline of their influence, just as that of the true merchant had declined a century earlier. At the mid-century, therefore, to create a successful commission business was the aim of ambitious young men in trade. The willingness of the leather manufacturers to employ the Booths in this way was, as they themselves recognized, the result 'simply (of) having a good name, and so long as we keep that good name we shall never be without a large consignment business in skins, for if one man falls off another will take his place.'

The immediate result of the need to maintain this 'good name', and of the entry into shipping, was a change in the personal plans of the two brothers. The known reliability and sound judgment of the elder brother was an asset of increasing value, while the management of the steamers was the particular field of the younger one. It was thus agreed that Alfred Booth should extend his stay in New York. The position was stated with youthful candour by Charles. 'I want you to understand,' he wrote, 'that as far as the living goes, I would as soon be out at New York as here, and in fact look forward to coming out. It is only for the good of the business that I wish to stay here. You are much more reliable to act for yourself and for other people than I am, and you would find it much harder to send me business than I you. On the other hand, I have much more push and more friends.' It was not until after his marriage to Miss Lydia Butler in 1867 that Alfred Booth returned home; and he made his last prolonged stay in America from 1869 to 1871. From then until his retirement in 1887, he remained at Liverpool as the senior partner, primarily interested in the American business. As events turned out, the difficult first years of the steamship venture kept Charles Booth at home, and the active management of the New York house became increasingly the work of the junior partners. The first of these was Thomas Fletcher, their cousin and close friend, who, after being trained as an engineer, joined the firm in 1867. Shrewd and hardworking, his mind and personality were excellent foils for those of the two brothers; being more forthright and robust. 'I hope,' wrote Charles Booth to him in 1871, with regard to a letter despatched to the Turneys of Nottingham, 'it does not partake of the usual fault of my lucubrations, too (much) damned ingenuity.' The fourth partner, Henry Romilly, joined the firm in 1870.[1] For much of his sixteen years with Alfred Booth and Company he was a sick man, and he appears in the partnership books as a more shadowy figure than his colleagues. He was primarily concerned with the finances of the business, although he spent most of the 'seventies in America.

While the twenty years which followed 1865—as will be shown—formed an epoch in the history of the firm, they were also distinctive years in the social activities of the two brothers.

[1] The Honourable Henry Romilly was the son of the first Lord Romilly and grandson of Sir Samuel Romilly. His sister married Henry, second son of Mr Justice Crompton, and first cousin of Alfred and Charles Booth.

Once permanently settled at home, Alfred Booth resumed with vigour his interest in art and history, as well as renewing his close connection with the affairs of the Renshaw Street Chapel, of which he was Congregational Treasurer from 1875 to 1883. With Charles Booth these years are divided into two periods by a serious breakdown in health, which kept him away from the business in 1874-5. During the first of these periods, he worked actively with the more radical elements in the social and political life of the city of Liverpool. With Francis Greg, he represented Liverpool on the executive committee of the Education League in the controversies over the Education Act of 1870, explaining to his brother that his policy was to conciliate the parsons, although 'we will have our revenge some day, but it is the only way to get the bill through.' He participated in the Legal Aid Society, the Toxteth Association and the Liverpool Operatives Trades Hall, of which he was a director. 'I like the men one gets amongst in this way, they have a sort of charm about them, being much more simple-minded and unsophisticated than most of us.' When the Franco-Prussian War broke out in 1870, he noted, 'The French seem to be the worst offenders entirely, but I believe Bismarck is as great a scoundrel as anybody.' He prophesied the German victory and thought that Napoleon would be dead or in London within six months. His marriage in April of the following year, to Miss Mary Macaulay, daughter of Charles Zachary Macaulay (brother of the historian), brought him not only under the influence of his wife's father but into closer contact with the 'solid phalanx' of her cousins, the Potter family. These included Beatrice Webb, and among the husbands of her many sisters, Leonard Courtney, later Lord Courtney of Penwith, Alfred Cripps, later Lord Parmoor, Henry Hobhouse, and Daniel Meinertzhagen, a London banker. Many of these were to have a profound effect upon his later work. The second period began with his return to England in 1875, after a prolonged rest in Switzerland. It was not, however, until the end of 1877 that he recommenced his business life, and then in London rather than in Liverpool. With the particular needs of the firm's leather interests in view, he opened an office in 84, King William Street. It is from this date that the London connection of Alfred Booth and Company originates.

During these years, although there was growth, the general character of the American business altered little: and this remained true until the beginning of the 1890's. The general commission work, so eagerly sought after in the early days of the firm, continued. In the late 'sixties, tinplate, soda ash, hops and even paper, were sold in New York for English manufacturers; American bonds were bought and sold on the instructions of various friends; and a fair amount of ship's husbandry was undertaken in connection with Liverpool-owned vessels calling at New York. But the main interest of the firm became increasingly concerned with light leather, and in this their business was 'a retail business basing its claim to profits on special work and special knowledge of what we deal in'.

The opportunity for this type of middleman arose from the fact that the average leather producing and manufacturing unit, on both sides of the Atlantic, was small and that it used a wide range of raw materials. In the total value of their output, these industries had long been major elements in the British and American economies. In eighteenth century England, leather was reputed to rank second only to wool in the numbers of workpeople employed in its fabrication: at the middle of the nineteenth century, according to the economist Mc-Culloch, its magnitude was equal to that of the iron industry, and was surpassed only by the two great textiles, cotton and wool. The number of people in these islands who were employed on the diverse activities associated with leather, had risen from 254,000 in 1839 to 400,000 in 1870. But the size of the characteristic establishments in the Northamptonshire boot and shoe industry, in the glove-making shops of the West Country, Worcestershire and around Nottingham, in the ubiquitous saddle and harness manufacture, and even in the widespread tanning and fellmongering, remained not far removed from that of 'Simon the Tanner, whose home was by the seashore at Joppa'.[2] As late as 1880, the average tanner employed 18 persons, and there were many smaller firms. Much the same could be said of the American leather industries. The famous McKay machine for sewing the uppers and soles of

[2] J. H. Clapham, *An Economic History of Modern Britain*, Vol. II, p. 36.

boots and shoes had been introduced shortly before the Civil War but, until the 'eighties, progress towards factory organization of any size was small.

In supplying the American market with sheepskin leather, Alfred Booth and Company, at this period, stood on the periphery of the English trade in this commodity. Geographically, the industry was organized from London, where Bermondsey had long been the centre of the largest English tanners and leather dressers, and where the leather merchants and factors were grouped in the area of Mincing Lane. The bulk of the leather exports, amounting to about £2,500,000 in the 'sixties, consisted of boots and shoes, sent mainly to the newly-developing British dependencies, Australia, Canada, South Africa and the West Indies. Even in finished leather, the main markets were, and remained, in France, Germany, Holland and Belgium. In 1860, the export of sheepskins was valued at £250,000, although the amount was to grow in the next fifteen years. Thus the trade to the U.S.A. in this commodity was a major branch neither of British exports generally nor of the leather industries in particular. Finished leather goods were effectively shut out of the American market by high tariffs, and the import of tanned and untanned skins permitted only because domestic supplies failed to meet the demand for leather goods. It was thus a highly specialized trade, and well could Alfred Booth say that two young men in their circumstances might be expected to have sought their careers in some more general field of English economic activity.

As factors, Alfred Booth and Company offered two services: first an organization by which the American manufacturer could obtain, economically, the type of sheepskin he particularly required, and, secondly, the provision of credit to the small firms with whom they dealt on both sides of the Atlantic. Both required a great deal of skill and acumen. In the first of these services, where American dealers employed the firm to buy special brands or types of skins, the matter was straightforward and presented no difficulties. In March, April and May, 1873, for example, such special orders averaged £5,000 respectively, representing a third of the firm's total monthly shipments. It was rather in the sale of English consigned skins that the specialized knowledge was required. Here the basic policy of the business was laid down as: 'It is not in our interest to get the better of either the men we buy from or those we sell to—but to do the best we can for each subject to a moderate remuneration for ourselves, and to give our chief attention to getting the utmost value out of the goods we deal in (1) by proper preparation and (2) by bringing the skins into use for the purpose they best suit.' A sales policy had thus to be formulated which was justified by the advantages accruing to Alfred Booth and Company's clients. To achieve such success, however, was no easy matter. It involved the assessment of the probable future course of prices in two markets, the English and the American, which, although connected, often moved independently of one another. That in the United States tended to be volatile, and was characterized by marked seasonal activity; most purchases being made in the autumn and spring. In England, on the other hand, the price of the primary product —such as untanned pickled pelts—depended upon the domestic and export demand for finished leather, whether in the form of goods or not. It was also powerfully influenced by the price of wool because, from the fellmonger's point of view, wool and skins were joint products.

In reaching a policy based on these two sets of data, the governing factor was the cost at which the English supplier could replace the stock sold in America. As Charles Booth explained, 'the ordinary principle and theory of business is that we hold the stock of salted goods and the manufacturers buy as they want to keep their works going, and hold the stocks of finished goods. If they buy beforehand, it can only be because they think that when they want the goods they will have to pay more for them, and if the market is going up, it can only pay us to let them hold the stock instead of us if we can get the goods replaced at the price we are paid. That is, if prices go up 30% in two years, it is better for us and for our friends if we make the advance on a succession of shipments and more the better, than if we held all the time to the same (stock). If we wished to sell in large lots and will make some concession to do so, it can only be because we think prices are going down and are satisfied we can replace as low as we can sell, or it is because we need the money and cannot afford to hold. Then there is the time when prices are at the bottom, when if it lasts long enough it may be both to our interest to sell and to the buyers to buy goods for which they have no immediate need —it being for their interest to hold stock and ours to sell as long as we can put ourselves, by replacing, in as good a position as if we had held. This is simply because after a while goods are better held tanned than salted.'

As a sales organization, the firm had the additional and important task of advising their regular customers on the reaction of buyers to their particular products. The output of even the same tanner or fellmonger varied considerably, partly because of the empirical character of the techniques employed, partly because of changes in the quality of the skins. Much therefore depended upon the habits of the workmen. 'Johnstone was here yesterday,' wrote Alfred Booth in July, 1868, 'and mentioned the annoyance and loss he has to contend with because of men going off to drink on a sudden and leaving their work to spoil. He has just had £20 worth of pelts spoilt through three men going off last Monday morning. This work especially in warm weather has to be carried through, or injury of some kind is bound to be done . . . Johnstone is this time bringing them up before a magistrate, he says he cannot afford it any longer.' For these reasons, some skins were soft, white and supple, but went bad quickly : others kept indefinitely but did not make good leather when tanned in bark : yet again, others took a great deal of sumac in tanning and were thus expensive to work. By visits or by letter, advice was offered to the offending establishment; occasionally even the technical assistance of the larger manufacturers was enlisted to help smaller clients. In periods of dull trade, further advice was given on the sorting of skins into various sizes, a 'generous' assortment facilitating sales in New York.

With regard to the second service provided by the firm—the provision of credit—suppliers of skins generally received three-quarters of the invoice value of their goods on delivery at the warehouse, paid in cash or by bill of exchange. Regular customers might, in times of financial difficulty, be helped by advances while the goods were still in the process of production.

Accounts were settled at regular intervals, or in the case of casual clients, when the particular transaction was completed. In America, skins were sold on ten, or at the most, thirty, days credit in the early 'sixties. By the end of the decade, however, these terms had lengthened considerably. Thirty days became a minimum, sixty common, and ninety days an occasional occurrence. Later, in the middle of the eighteen seventies, when trade was dull, four months' credit was not unusual, with a discount of 1% per month for cash. In this way, a considerable amount of money was employed in financing American leather manufacturers and dressers; and the control of these advances, on both sides of the Atlantic, was an important aspect of the business. In England, when sales were slow, large sums might be advanced against temporarily unsaleable stocks of skins, thus absorbing a dangerous proportion of the firm's capital. Further, sales below invoiced prices might leave the tanner or fell-monger heavily in debt to the factor. The recovery of debt so created was one of the ways in which Alfred Booth and Company were later forced into the manufacturing side of the industry, both in England and America.

Associated with the financial aspect of the business, although not of direct concern to the consignors, was the problem of remitting money from America between 1863 and 1878. During these years the dollar had no fixed gold value, and there were considerable fluctuations in the dollar/sterling rate of exchange. As skins were valued in sterling and sold in dollars, there were thus opportunities for profits, and risks of loss, in the way in which one currency was exchanged into another. As the company bore the risks, it was assumed that the profits should be theirs also; although not without some misgivings, for Charles Booth often thought it wrong 'to sell in currency and not give the seller his option of holding for his exchange'. There were years in which losses were incurred, but generally these exchange transactions showed a small profit. The general principle adopted in this matter was that the cost of sterling in terms of dollars was highest at midsummer and lowest at Christmas. 'This is quite natural as it is in the late Spring and early Summer that cotton and other things come to an end for shipping and the heaviest export of gold takes place,' wrote Alfred

Booth. 'I know the English bankers always used to make their arrangements for a higher rate of exchange in the Spring and Summer and a lower one in the Fall and Winter.' Success followed from the observance of this rule and from the judicious purchase of gold. The worst fluctuations occurred in the 'sixties, coming to an end with the failure of the corner in gold in September, 1869. The gold premium rose to 162 points and then fell sharply to 132, 'which made me feel good', noted Charles Booth; 'I think this is the last squeak of the gold brokery and it must squeeze them confoundedly . . . I would have given £5 to be in Broad Street yesterday (24th September). It must have been splendid and I think will cure their taste for corners for a while, as they have constructed a very narrow one and been jammed into it themselves.' This forecast was correct. Fluctuations continued until a gold standard was resumed on January 1, 1879, but never on the scale of the previous seven years.

For these services, Alfred Booth and Company charged a commission, in addition to the costs of transporting the goods between the warehouse in Liverpool and the cellars at 57, Broad Street, New York. During the Civil War, the full commission was 5%, with an additional 2½% *del credere* for the assumption of risks of bad debts. With the end of the war the latter was reduced to 1%, making the total charge 6%. The use of the telegraph, laid across the Atlantic in 1866, and of steam ships, by speeding the communication of information and the transport of goods, lessened the difficulties of overseas trade. As a consequence, by 1871, regular clients paid only 5%, the company carrying the possibility of bad debts: chance shippers, however, were still required to pay the higher rate. The only change during the next fifteen years was to make 5% the charge for all clients. When advances were not required, there was a reduction of 2—2½% on the commission, the actual amount tending to vary with the rate of interest commonly charged for loans.

The basis of a transatlantic business of this kind was the transmission of accurate information, and for this the presence of a partner, at first temporarily, and later permanently, resident in New York, was a great advantage. When Alfred Booth and Company was founded, long letters were written by the two brothers almost every day. In the tradition of mercantile correspondence, they contained not only business matters, comments on contemporaries and customers, but also long statements on political events in England and America. As the staff grew, this correspondence was divided into the regular 'house letter', read by the senior clerks, and the 'partners' letter' which contained confidential information. Later, the miscellaneous items of news became less frequent and the letters achieved what Thomas Fletcher called the 'dull heights of Booth and Company's officialism'; but these *obiter dicta* never entirely disappeared as is shown by the partnership letters of the nineteen-twenties and 'thirties. The use of the telegraph was quickly adopted, and one of Henry Romilly's first tasks on joining the firm in 1870 was the construction of a telegraphic code. By the end of the century, as Alfred Booth and Company's interests grew in various parts of the world, there was a constant stream of correspondence between London, Liverpool, America, Brazil, Australia, New Zealand and India.

The expansion of the business, for which this organization was gradually built up, was at first slow. Despite the addition of shipowning and the Holts' forwarding agency, a warehouseman, two clerks and a new partner sufficed to meet the needs of the Liverpool office in 1867—making six in all; while in New York there was a partner, two clerks and a warehouseman.[3] American sales in 1868 remained unchanged at between £2,000 and £2,500 a month, although with Alfred Booth's increasing knowledge of skins, losses resulting from bad valuations had begun to disappear. Miscellaneous commission work and some shipping business brought in a further small income. The bulk of the skin shipments from Liverpool continued in the form of grains and fleshes, but with an increasing quantity of pickled foreign sheepskins, technically called foreign roans.

It was upon this latter commodity that the expansion of the business in the subsequent years of this period primarily depended. It reflected the increasing demand for boots and shoes in America—between 1860 and 1890 the population doubled—

[2] The clerks at Liverpool were C. J. Garland and G. R. Heise; whose son became a director of the Booth Steamship Company and lives in retirement at Hoylake, near Liverpool. A. E. Gaenslen and F. Lingelbach were the clerks in New York.

the production of which far outstripped domestic supplies of leather. 'Boston is a good staple trade,' stated Alfred Booth in 1870, 'as the Americans must have boots and we must find them the leather as not . . .' That England was able to provide part of this demand for skins was largely due to the upward movement in the price of wool, which made the plucking of wool from imported sheepskins a profitable business. Under the stimulus of a cotton shortage, wool imports for 1865-69 were 41% higher than in the previous quinquennium; and wool imports for 1880-84 were double those for 1865-69. This movement in wool imports was paralleled by the increase in the number of raw sheepskins brought into the country. During the eighteen sixties the quantity had doubled to reach 3,500,000 in 1869; and in the rising prosperity of the early years of the next decade imports reached 7,500,000 in 1874. From this peak there was a slight decline in the next six years. The pelt, which was a joint product of fellmongering, was thus available at low prices for tanning. In many cases too thin for splitting, the skins were admirably suited for use in the boot and shoe industry. These foreign roans were exported in pickle and tanned on the other side of the Atlantic. After 1870, and until the growing supplies of American sheepskins in the last decade of the century made the trade unprofitable, they formed the main element in the firm's leather business.

A market for foreign roans was opened up by Alfred Booth in the early years of the company's existence through a series of fortnightly visits from New York to Boston, then the centre of the boot and shoe industry. After 1868, and especially after the autumn of 1869, the trade grew rapidly. 'We are doing a smashing business in skins,' wrote Charles Booth enthusiastically in 1870, when sales had reached a peak of £8,000 a month; and the growing predominance of footwear manufacturers among their clients led naturally, in November of that year, to the establishment of a branch in Boston. Accommodation was found in 141, Purchase Street, and Mr Gaenslen, the salesman at New York, was promoted manager under the control of the resident partner at 57, Broad Street. Three years later total sales had reached £16,000 a month, and by 1880 Alfred Booth and Company were perhaps the most important suppliers of pickled sheepskins to the American market, having almost a monopoly of the trade to Boston. Some idea of the relative importance of this article in the shipments from Liverpool to the firm's house in the United States can be obtained from the sales for the last fortnight in July 1880, which were: 41 casks of fleshes, 76 of grains and 697 of foreign roans.

It was partly because of the growth of the foreign roan business and partly because of the increasing number of commissions for goatskins, that Charles Booth opened his London office. For the search for suitable sheepskins led to supplies being obtained from Belgian and French tanners and fellmongers. Contact with such men was best made through the London leather and skin sales which they attended. Before 1877, when the office was opened, one of the partners had made regular visits to London; now the time had arrived for the establishment of permanent quarters.

The advances made during the 'seventies were consolidated in the face of some difficulties in the period 1880-1885. The impression gained from the partnership letter-books is that while the volume of trade was maintained, profit margins shrank. 1875, 1876, 1879, 1880 and 1882 were particularly bad years, as they indeed were in other branches of trade and industry. Split skins were more affected than roans, owing in part to greater competition from American importing merchants, and in part to the fact that the demand for footwear was less subject to variation than that for gloves and other goods made from fleshes and grains. To the fall in the sales of these types of skins was added, in 1879, the accumulation of large stocks of roans through a misjudgment of the market, and first Charles and then Alfred Booth went out to America to investigate the state of the business. As a result of their visits a tighter control was instituted over the Boston branch, and in an attempt to increase the sales of split sheepskins in New York, showrooms were opened in the neighbourhood of the 'Swamp' so as to be near the buyers of leather. Room was found in Frankfort Street, in a building partly occupied by the staff of the newspaper *Volks Zeitung*; here, samples were made available while the main offices and cellars remained at Broad Street. At home, the same cause led to the establishment of the Nuneaton Leather

D

Company, in partnership with a Nuneaton tanner, Mr Johnson. By this means it was hoped to produce heavy grains of a type which would particularly meet the needs of the New York market. These skins were to be sold under the trade name of ABC, the other products of the tannery being distributed through other trade channels.

The establishment of the Nuneaton Leather Company in 1882 was not, however, the first step which Alfred Booth and Company had taken in the direction of the manufacturing side of the leather industry. An arrangement had been involuntarily entered into in America some five years earier, which was to have the most profound influence on the fortunes of the company. In 1877 Messrs. Kent and Stevens, tanners and leather dressers, of Gloversville, came to a stop as a result of frauds practised by the second partner, Stevens. John Kent, the other member of the partnership, was a man of great technical ability, who today, because of his 'fatliquoring' process and 'Dongola'[4] tannage, is regarded as one of the outstanding pioneers of the American leather industry : both innovations forming part of a long search for a method of producing cheap kid leather to replace the expensive products imported from France and used in the Gloversville glove trade. When the frauds were discovered, the partnership owed Booth and Company $70,000 for South African deerskins and Brazilian goatskins supplied them. To save this sum and to help Kent, for whose ability Alfred and Charles Booth had a high regard, the company paid off the other creditors and secured its advances by a mortgage on the factory. Two years later, the relations between the two concerns became closer, when it was agreed that Booth and Company should extend its interests into the field of dried skins, particularly those of goat and kangaroo, and

[4] 'Dongola' tannage was the application of an old principle of making leather partly by tanning with alum and partly with vegetable materials, initially used in producing an imitation glazed kid. It was so named because it was developed during the Egyptian War of 1881-1885. Fatliquoring involved the treatment of the skin in an emulsion of soap and oil. 'It was the application of the method of "fat-liquoring" by James (sic) Kent to his Dongola tannage which gave them (combination tannages) the place they now possess, by providing a cheap substitute for egg-yolk, and enabling the tanner to obtain softness and resistance to water without producing the greasy feel which is common to curried leathers.' E. H. Procter, *The Principles of Leather Manufacture*, pp. 375-6.

that the Gloversville factory should be worked jointly by John Kent and Booth and Company. Under this arrangement, Julius Kuttner, who joined the staff of Booth and Company in 1873, and upon whose name and that of his wife the mortgage was held, went to Gloversville to superintend the commercial side of the business, leaving Kent free to concentrate on its experimental and technical aspects. By 1880, Booth and Company were buying large quantities of Ceará goatskins, and the leather —an imitation kid—was sold as 'Daisy Kid'. When, later in the year, Charles Booth visited Gloversville, the plant was enlarged by the purchase of the adjoining Dodge factory for the sum of $30,000. The success of 'Daisy Kid' led to the application of 'Dongola' tannage to kangaroo skins and by early 1882 $262,000 was employed in the factory, represented largely by goods in the process of production. At the same date, the total sales of sheepskins in New York and Boston amounted to £200,000 or about a million dollars annually.

It was from this, as yet, small business in kid leather that the second stage of Alfred Booth and Company's leather interests was to grow. In the quarter of a century which had elapsed since 1865, the American business had developed, not perhaps spectacularly, but with increasing strength and stability. The foundation of the Nuneaton Leather Company in 1882, the outright purchase of the Gloversville factory on the death of John Kent in 1886; the appointment in 1887, in conjunction with Richard Young and Company, of an agent, Mr Miller, at Sidney to buy kangaroo skins; the peak exports from England of foreign roans between 1888 and 1892, with its growing element of New Zealand pelts; together mark a clearly defined stage in this development. In 1890, therefore, Alfred Booth and Company, with its New York house of Booth and Company, was a relatively small but well-established Anglo-American concern in the pickled pelt trade, with its largest market in the Boston boot and shoe industry. The total value of its business amounted to between £250,000 and £300,000 annually. In America, entrance had been made into the production of finished light leathers, more particularly for the manufacture of gloves, through the ownership of a tannery at Gloversville, Fulton County, New York.

CHAPTER IV

The Booth Line
1865-1881

While the fifteen years between 1865 and 1880 had seen a substantial growth of Alfred Booth and Company's leather trade, they represented a period of relative stagnation in shipping—the second of its major activities. Little change occurred in the volume of imports into, and exports from, the three North Brazilian ports, and a good deal of experimenting was required before the right type of vessel was found for the service.

The contracts for the two boats, which, it was thought would suffice for an adequate beginning in this branch of trade, were placed in February, 1865, with Hart and Sinnot, whose yards were situated near the Queen's Dock, Liverpool. The construction of the engines was entrusted to a firm new to this type of engineering, John Taylor and Company of Birkenhead, steam winch manufacturers, whose tender quoted the low figure of £2,280 for each engine. The ships themselves were built at £17 a ton, and the total sum involved was approximately £40,000. In accordance with the practice adopted by Alfred Holt, the iron hulls were nearly a quarter lighter in weight than was required for Lloyds class A ships, but stronger in the rivetting and trapping. The first of these vessels, the *Augustine*. was a three-decked, schooner-rigged, screw-driven ship of 1,056 gross tons, with registered dimensions of 213 feet x 29½ feet x 25 feet. The second ship, the *Jerome*, was of much the same size, but was brigantine-rigged and had only two decks. The engines, of the new compound type developed by Alfred Holt, were of 95 horse power. They were thus medium-sized craft, about half as big as the passenger and mail boats engaged in the Liverpool-New York run, or the largest ocean-going sailing ships. Like most other steamers of the period they were designed to carry both cargo and passengers.

The choice of these somewhat unusual names—*Augustine* and *Jerome*—had been the subject of long discussions among the family and their immediate circle of friends in Prince's Park. With characteristic optimism Charles Booth had written to his brother, 'I do like a set of men better than anything else and there should be a set of which there are plenty. We need not come to Joe Smith but I have no objection to *Hildebrand*.' The final decision lay between the Knights of the Round Table and the great figures of the Church. Emily Booth wanted the Knights; Anna Holt, John Crompton and Charles Booth the divines. And it was perhaps typical of their cultivated Nonconformist background that the majority should have favoured the religious figures because they 'were more solid'. So it was that the ships of the Booth Line acquired their distinctive names, of which *Hildebrand, Augustine, Jerome, Ambrose, Polycarp* and *Dominic* were typical.

The *Augustine* was launched late in 1865, advertised to depart on February 14, 1866, and Captain John Jackson appointed her first commander. She left Liverpool a day late, with 571 tons of coal and 57 tons of cargo, mainly fine goods. 'People have hardly believed she would go as advertised and the opposition are doing all they know. F. Lyon and Bros. are actually forced to ship under an assumed name because Singlehursts threaten to shut out their goods. Whom the Gods would destroy they first dement, so much for Singlehursts.' At Lisbon an additional 260 tons of cargo were obtained and two extra passengers. Charles Booth was aboard, and his account of the voyage was an augury of future troubles.

'We left Liverpool on the 15th,' he wrote, 'delayed to the last moment with the engines and got away from Bell Buoy at noon. A slow day down channel with the wind more or less against us, and then we set our square sails and had a gale aft all the way to Lisbon, where we arrived on the evening of the 20th with the engines on the last gasp—one of the pumps broken, etc. It took two days to get this mended and off we went and got to Ceará in 17 days. The passage should be done in 15 days and we had a fair passage as to weather. We broke down once entirely and stopped nine hours. Two days did us at Ceará, where we had the agent doing all he could to hinder us and everybody else all they could to facilitate us. We left again on the evening of the 14th (March) and were in Maranham on the morning of the 17th (Saturday). Away again on Sunday afternoon, and here (Pará) on the 21st, one day later on the whole. Here, 84 tons of cargo were obtained and on revisiting the first two ports, a further 590 tons. Homeward from Ceará, the voyage took 20 days. I do not think we can average much, if anything, shorter, it is the 600/700 miles one has to go round to keep the sails on across the trades—that one goes north until you are in 25°/30° north at this time of the year. That done we made our easting fast.' The journey from Lisbon took another 6½ days, and the returning ship was off the estuary of the Mersey in the first days of May, where her sister-ship, the *Jerome*, was seen undergoing trials. The round voyage of 9,500 miles had taken three months, of which sixty days had been spent at sea. Some 450 tons of coal had been used and the vessel had averaged 6.84 knots per hour. The cost of the voyage amounted to £1,850, of which the major items were £329 for port charges, £498 for provisions, £401 for coals and £495 for wages. Subsequent voyage costs appear to have been about a third higher, although the proportions of the various components remained roughly the same.

Financially, the result was a loss of £3 on the costs of the voyage. There were, however, some gains to offset this initial loss. The prospect of steam communication with Europe had been received with great enthusiasm by the commercial communities of the three ports. At Pará—'a go-ahead place—quite Yankee in tone—the same overweening conceit based on the same confidence in their future'—and at Maranham the arrival of the *Augustine* had been celebrated by music and fireworks. In the first flush of excitement the principal merchants discussed the possibility of a regular mail service, which the young shipowner offered to provide in return for an annual subsidy of 100,000 reis (£10,000) to be paid jointly by the three provinces concerned. But irrespective of this plan, the visit made it clear that a strong initial hold upon the trade could be obtained only by more frequent sailings than could be provided by two ships. As a consequence, the *Cleator* was chartered from the Holts until a third vessel could be built. In the meantime, with the

Jerome, which sailed on her maiden voyage on May 15, 1866, under the command of Captain Hutcheson, the three ships could provide a monthly departure from Liverpool.

By the middle of 1866, however, discussions in the assemblies of Pará, Maranham and Ceará made it evident that the subsidy required for a monthly service from each of their main ports would not be forthcoming. Accordingly, Charles Booth submitted a modified proposal in December, 1866, by which a monthly departure from Liverpool (via Lisbon) to Pará, Maranham and Ceará, was planned, with a return voyage by the same route, during the first seven months of the year. From August to December, the return journey along the north Brazilian coast was omitted, and the homeward voyage commenced from the last outward port of call, Ceará. The firm would not bind itself to a particular day of arrival at Pará, but expected to cover the outward journey in 22 days with the *Augustine* and *Jerome* and in 24 days with the *Cleator*. 'The arrangement of the voyages is that which after the experience we have had presents itself to us as the best both for the trade and ourselves, and we believe the interests are identical. It also makes it easier to work the trade with three boats by shortening the voyages during the Autumn. So far as Pará is concerned you have all the year round the direct arrivals from Europe and you have direct departures to Europe during the season of the crop and during the months when there are most passengers homewards. The loss on the homeward freight from Ceará during crop season by returning to the North is too considerable to be faced without a larger subsidy, amounting as it would to $\frac{1}{4}$d. per lb. or from £300 to £500 for each of five voyages.' The final outcome of the negotiations appears to have been the grant of an annual subsidy amounting in all to a few thousand pounds, in return for a monthly service from Liverpool, via Lisbon to Pará, Maranham and Ceará, and thence home via Lisbon.

Despite the subsidy, heavy losses were incurred until 1868-9. With only a small leather business, these were years of financial stringency, in which much depended upon the credits given them by the Holts and the Rathbones, and, until its closure in 1868, the Royal Bank of Liverpool. 'The fact is,' wrote Charles Booth, 'that we are running our business with other people's

money and especially Royal Bank money.' This lack of success
was, in the circumstances, not surprising. After the financial
disasters of the preceding year, 1867 saw the end of a long and
costly war between Brazil and Paraguay, which had led to a
30% depreciation of Brazilian currency in terms of sterling,
had depleted supplies of labour for the coffee, sugar and cotton
plantations, and had also 'largely reacted on Portugal, the
wealthier and trading classes of which are dependent in no
small degree on Brazil for a large part of their income'. It was
thus difficult to find work for the ships on the Liverpool/North
Brazilian route, and consequently both the *Jerome* and the
Augustine were employed on chartered voyages in 1867, and
the *Jerome* again in the following year.

But there were other factors in the situation of a less temporary nature. Until the end of the 'seventies the amount of
freight to be carried did not increase greatly. The basis of the
trade lay in the cotton shipments, mainly from Ceará but in
smaller quantities from Maranham also. Sugar from these ports
is first mentioned as a large element in freights in 1875, and
coffee five years later. It was only occasionally that nuts, drugs
and rubber from Pará provided a greater revenue than cotton;
although the earnings from the cargoes obtained here were
almost always greater than from Maranham. But with keen
competition from sailing vessels, there was no certainty of an
adequate homeward cargo and the journey along the coast from
Pará to Ceará—a distance of some seven to eight hundred miles
—was often very necessary. The position at Liverpool was, in
this respect, easier. In practice, the volume of homeward freight
was always greater than that outwards in these years, although
there was little difference in their contributions to the earnings
of the voyage. The rapid expansion of North Brazil dates from
the end of the 'seventies and was associated with the development of rubber in the Amazon Basin and with a flow of emi-
grants. It is only from this date that outward cargoes began to
dominate the freight position, reflecting the import into Brazil
of such things as stone, railway and power equipment and
coal.

In the second place, although steamers were quicker than
sailing ships, their higher freight charges placed them at a dis-

advantage in handling low-value cargo for which rapidity of carriage was not an important factor. The necessity of calling at Lisbon, as well as at Maranham, Ceará and Pará, also meant that sailing vessels plying directly between any one of these ports and Europe, often did the journey in a shorter time. The fact that the compound engine remained in an experimental stage for nearly a decade after its initial development by Alfred Holt accentuated this disadvantage. 'Steamship owning,' commented Charles Booth in 1869, 'seems to be a constant succession of unfathomable and costly experiments and can only be carried on when there are large earnings coming in.' This was the price paid for the empirical character of technical advance —'the fact is, A.H. does everything by rule of thumb which comes right if he is always at it'; but rarely if he contented himself with general directions. The main defect of the high-pressure engines lay in their boilers, and the *Augustine* and *Jerome* had been in commission but nine months when these had to be replaced at a total cost of £3,200. The new ones were multitubular, having 200 square feet of additional heating surface. Even then experiment and adaptation continued: captains, mates and engineers were switched from one vessel to another in an endeavour to find the most economical method of working them. This plethora of mechanical troubles was not limited to the Holts and the Booths, but was a feature of the early stages of steamship development. In 1867, for example, all the ships of the Guion Line lost their propellers. Thus early steamship owners were required to be conversant with the technical, as well as the commercial, side of the business. 'We do not understand the priming you mention,' complained the young manager to the captain of the *Jerome*, 'as it seems quite unaccountable: and we are not satisfied about the stopping 3 or 4 hours to cool bearings, we never have heard of such a thing being necessary and it seems like either carelessness or idleness on the part of the engineers . . . We wish them to try the experiment of letting some air into the combustion chamber at the back of the furnaces as we are of the opinion that this will improve the draught . . . The holes can be bored so as to be filled up again if they do not do any good.' By the end of the 'seventies these initial troubles had been overcome, and the ex-

tent of the subsequent improvement can be gauged from the
following figures : —

TABLE I

Year	Ship	Gross Tonnage	Speed Knots per hr.	Distance per day	Coal Consumption Per 10 knot run Cwts	Per day Tons
1880	Jerome	1,096	7.88	189 knots	10.33	9.7
	Augustine	1,106	8.21	197 knots	10.5	10.4
1892	Lanfranc	1,657	10.33	250 knots	20.2	25
	Origen	1,541	8.5	200 knots	16	16
1908	Hilary	6,325	13.4	322 miles	53.2	77–85
	Gregory	2,030	7.64	183 miles	19	17

Cheap coal was clearly a fundamental element in the development of the British mercantile navy, quite apart from the
role it played as a bulk outward cargo. During the first decade
of the present century the Booth Steamship Company often
bought large Dowlais coal at 13s. a ton f.o.b. Cardiff, and
never at more than 16s.; which compared favourably with the
first coals purchased in 1866 at slightly under 14s. a ton.

It was in dealing with these early technical problems that the
partnership found their close association with Philip and Alfred
Holt of such great value. It was under the aegis of these two
men that the Booth Line was created, and the relationship between it and the Holts' Ocean Steamship Company remained
an intimate one. Until 1873, it was the engineers of the latter
company who maintained the four vessels managed and partly
owned by Alfred Booth and Company. In that year Edward
Crompton, then at Alexandria, was appointed the first super-
intendent-engineer of the line, and from that date onward the
firm had the advice of its own technical staff.

The experience of these early years dispelled the sanguine
hopes, earlier entertained, of a quick and decisive victory over
sailing ships in the North Brazilian trade. With so tenuous a
margin of economic superiority, the brothers now looked to
increased steam tonnage as the means by which the older type
of craft could be superseded. A few steamships could never hope
to command the freight market from the Brazilian ports, but a
large number of such ships might succeed in crowding out the
sailing vessels. With considerable foresight, they argued that
competition would lie between steam and sail, rather than be-

tween rival steamship companies in the same trade. Hence the building of three ships by the Singlehursts in 1869 and of two by Hugh Evans and Company's Maranham Steamship Company in the following year caused them less anxiety than it did many of their contemporaries; some of whom prophesied the end of their venture. 'As we approach the Singlehurst opposition it seems more and more likely that it will be only competition which in some senses will prove to be a combination.' Although denied an outstanding success, their three years start was not without advantage. Experience had been gained in the running of steamships and a connection formed. By good fortune, in the last year before the Singlehursts' opposition 'the steamers made £8,500 clear, which just makes up interest for the three years and gives them the start afresh and the trade established'. This connection included some of the older houses in the trade, of whom Gunston, Wilson and Company was the most important. This firm withdrew some of its sailing ships and by providing £10,000 made possible the building of two additional steamers. The first was the *Ambrose*—designed to replace the *Cleator*— a two-decked, brigantine-rigged, screw-driven vessel of 1,168 tons, constructed by Leslies of Newcastle-on-Tyne in 1868 for £16,000: with 90 h.p. engines made by Fawcett, Preston and Company for £3,500. The second was the *Bernard*, built in 1870 to carry the extra cargoes caused by the rising tide of prosperity. It was a smaller, schooner-rigged ship of 915 gross tons made by Royden and Fawcett of Liverpool, for £14 a ton, with two compound direct action engines provided by the same firm for £4,650. In this vessel, Alfred and Charles Booth held thirty-five sixty-fourths, of which twelve were in the hands of the builders as security for £3,000, which it was agreed to pay within two years.

More important than these advantages was the fact that 1869—when the first of the Singlehursts' steamships sailed— turned out to be the first of five prosperous years; which gave rise to the view that there was room for more than one company in the North Brazilian trade. When the *Ambrose* sailed on May 15, 1869, it had a 'ripping' cargo; 'there has been some little work connected with this,' commented Charles Booth with faint irony, 'and we were practically here all last night—Heise altogether and the rest of us (except Christopher Garland) went home for three hours. So you won't expect a long letter from me. I and Chris are the only denizens now.' As a consequence, when R. Singlehurst and Company were offered a plan of alternative departures from Liverpool, it was accepted; not, however, without the good offices of Gunston, Wilson and Company, who were financially interested in both groups of ships. Under this arrangement, the Singlehurst or Red Cross Line sailed on the 12th of each month and the steamers under Booth management on the 27th. With the third concern, the Maranham Steamship Company, relations were at first less happy, because of its desire to maintain a monopoly of the Maranham trade. The company's refusal to enter an agreement with regard to dates of sailing led to a 'freight war' between itself and the other two steamer interests. The contest, waged for nearly a year, ended in 1871 with a compromise scheme which, while providing for a closely integrated series of Liverpool departures, gave Hugh Evans and Company the sole right of running a direct service from Liverpool to Maranham. On the basis of this plan, the three lines worked amicably for the next thirty years.

Thus from the start, with formidable competition from sailing vessels, the popularly expected conflict in the North Brazilian steamer trade, was largely averted. Opposition, when it came, was provided by foreign companies; but even here, combination rather than competition was the outstanding feature. This was true of other Liverpool steamship routes also; the Holts, for example, had established a powerful 'ring or conference' in the China outward freight trade by the end of the 1870's. The tendency towards acting in concert was therefore inherent in the character of liner business. For in the absence of an indefinitely expanding trade and with a large capital investment, it was only possible to provide fixed sailings and freight rates—and thus calculable costs to the shipper—in return for regular custom. As a consequence, the bulk of Liverpool's trade between 1860 and 1910 'passed from ships engaged in the general carrying trade of the world, chartered by merchants for particular voyages, into the hands of regular Lines'. The proportion of the port's total trade thus handled increased from

64% to 79% in the period 1897-1910.[1] In the course of time, it was inevitable that the close association established in 1871 in the relatively small trade to the North Brazilian ports should lead to some form of amalgamation, especially having regard to the fact that each of the interests was really a form of partnership. With agreed working arrangements, the withdrawal or retirement of a predominant financial partner in one of the companies tended to weaken the position of the remaining lines. It was this position which resulted in the formation of the new Booth Steamship Company Limited in 1901. This event was foreshadowed thirty years earlier, when the provincial assembly of Pará offered a subsidy of £10,000 a year for a bi-monthly service to Manáos. The Singlehursts then proposed the joint management of the two lines under the control of Charles Booth, in order to include the new trade within the capacity of their eight ships. Nothing came of the proposal, however, because of his unwillingness to undertake the work without a full amalgamation of the two shipping interests. In the event, the Red Cross Line acquired the Manáos contract, which it operated until early in the 1880's.

The agreement made in 1871 between the three Liverpool houses covered a timetable of arrivals and departures, and an agreed scheme of outward freight rates. The basis of the timetable was a plan for three departures a month from England: the first going via Havre and Lisbon to Maranham and Pará, and returning the same way; the second, sailing to Lisbon and thence to Pará and Ceará, and home via Lisbon; the third also going to Lisbon and then to Maranham and Liverpool. By such an arrangement the three lines, with their ten ships, more than met the demands of the trade. Although altered slightly in 1876, this schedule remained until the end of the decade.

The position with regard to passenger and freight charges was somewhat more complicated. When the steamships were first employed on this route, the discovery of the correct rates had been a matter of trial and error. On the maiden voyage of the *Augustine* the outward rates had been frankly experimental, consisting of 70/- for fine and 35/- and 30/- for other categories of goods; cabin passengers were charged £40 and

[1] *Annual Report of the Liverpool Shipowners' Association.* 1910.

those who went steerage £18. These rates were soon found to be excessive, and by July, 1866, they had been reduced 'as a matter of policy in our opposition to sailing vessels'. In November of the same year, through rates from Havre had been dropped by a third, passenger fares from Lisbon to Pará by a half, the return fare made equivalent to a single fare and a half and the ticket made valid for twelve months. The first result of the combination with the Singlehursts in 1869 was the raising of these freight rates by 25%. After the struggle with the Maranham Steamship Company in 1870-71, a uniform series of charges was established which also remained unchanged until the end of the decade. At the three Brazilian ports, however, a looser hold was maintained on the trade. Here, homeward freight rates were left to the companies' agents, who made the best bargain they could with individual shippers. Sailing ships coming in for cotton and sugar during the crop season created a greater element of competition and it was often difficult to control the actions of the agents. Hence cotton, for example, brought home by the same ship, even from the same port, might be charged at a variety of rates. Of this homeward cargo, the highest rates were for rubber from Pará, which during the 'seventies brought in between 45/- and 47/- per ton measurement.

For the handling of homeward freight and passenger traffic the Brazilian agents of Alfred Booth and Company received 5% of all earnings; agents at Lisbon and Havre were also paid the same amount of commission. For traffic along the coast of South America 7½% of the receipts was given to the agents. Nothing was paid on disbursements made on ships' account; but during the years in which the various provincial assemblies granted the company a subsidy, the Brazilian agencies received 10% in the first year and 2½% thereafter. The firms originally appointed to undertake this work were F. G. da Costa and Fils, Pará; I. S. de Vasconcellos, Hughes & Company, Ceará; and I. D'O. Cantos & Col, Maranham. At Lisbon were Garland and Laidley, later to be Garland, Laidley and Company Limited, in which the Booth Steamship Company held an important interest. At Havre the agent for many years was J. M. Currie.

The fortunes of the four ships managed by Alfred Booth and

Company during these years are shown in the following table: —

TABLE II

Cargoes in Tons Measurement
(Except charter voyages)

	Outwards	Homewards		Outwards	Homewards
1866	1,540	5,248	1874	10,428	17,244
1867	1,567	7,284	1875	8,689	16,603
1868	3,932	10,528	1876	8,261	15,662
1869	11,100	13,618	1877	11,994	14,214
1870	13,073	13,083	1878	15,492	13,738
1871	11,882	19,192	1879	11,103	10,136
1872	13,744	20,092	1880	11,746	10,003
1873	10,640	13,500			

The vicissitudes of the early years are evident enough. Although arrears of interest were made up in 1868-9, another year was to elapse before the upward movement in earnings permitted the partial repayment of mortgages incurred in 1866-7, and the establishment of reserve and depreciation funds. Steamer earnings reached a peak during the Franco-Prussian War, 1870-1, and although the three succeeding years showed a decline from this high level, they were still very satisfactory. There was not only the volume of cargo to be carried, but also the advantages accruing from a regular scheme of sailings and higher freight rates. It was not until the second half of the decade that the widespread depression of the period showed itself in this particular trade. The results for 1875 and 1876 were extremely poor. But 1876 also proved to be a turning point: for from then onwards Brazilian trade made a marked recovery, especially that between South America and Portugal and France. Imports into the three provinces of Ceará, Maranham and Pará, which between 1872-6 had averaged £1,400,000, increased to £1,800,000 for the period 1882-6; and the respective exports figures from £1,950,000 to £2,500,000. Brazilian rubber production, although still small, grew by a third in the decade 1870-80. The gains from this extra freight were, however, limited by competition from foreign lines; but 1881 and 1882 were noted as exceptionally good years.

The first attempt to break into the carrying business to the three Brazilian ports was successfully countered in 1877, but at a cost of £5,000 to both Alfred Booth and Company and to R. Singlehurst and Company. More serious difficulties, however, soon made themselves evident as the upward movement of trade continued. By 1879, the shutting out of cargo at Havre and Lisbon, and of French inward freight at the Brazilian ports, led to increased efforts by the owners of sailing vessels and to a proposal to establish a French line based on Havre. At the same time, Pará, the most flourishing of the three ports, pressed for a faster and more frequent service to Europe. To this end, a French company, the Messageries Imperiales, was induced by means of a small subsidy of £4,000, to extend its service from France to Cayenne to include Pará on the homeward journey. Matters came to a head in July, 1879, when the Singlehursts were compelled, because of other commitments, to reduce their European departures. It was then recognized that it was 'hardly safe to go on longer in the steamship business from hand to mouth'.

The problem which thus presented itself had a dual aspect. With increasing commitments in the American leather business, there was the fundamental question of how desirable was the increased investment in shipping. Fifteen years' experience had shown that the employment of steamships in the North Brazilian trade was neither a very lucrative nor a smooth-running activity. On the other hand, with considerable deposits in the hands of the company and a large measure of prosperity in the leather business, there was no lack of capital. The Liverpool office was capable of dealing as well with eight as with four ships; and there was a feeling that building costs would rise. Secondly, an extension of the fleet to meet the needs of outward freight involved the question of finding adequate homeward cargoes. 'I suppose our experience has been,' wrote Alfred Booth, 'that a ship with considerable outward cargo can be made to pay by shifting ports for homeward cargo.' New homeward ports of call had therefore to be found. It was thus a matter of considerable discussion before the decision to increase their interest in shipping was made. Even so, some misgivings remained: 'I hope the North Brazil trade will prove worth sinking more money and trouble into,' commented Alfred Booth. 'I have not much heart for an opposition which is likely to take off the little cream there is in it and leave only work and worry more than ever.'

The solution of the problem was the work of Charles Booth.

During the latter part of 1879, and in 1880, temporary arrangements were made to deal with the immediate situation. These involved the purchase of two sailing ships, the *Bessie Dodd* and the *Carrie Dodd*, to carry gunpowder and other bulk cargo to Pará, returning with rubber and nuts direct to London. A more rigid timetable of ships' movements was enforced, including the cabling of departure dates from foreign ports, and efforts were made to handle more effectively French homeward cargoes. In the meantime, two outstanding difficulties disappeared. The Ceará cotton crop, which had failed in 1878, recovered its vitality, and the Messageries Imperiales, finding its service from Pará unprofitable, abandoned the project. The final plan evolved by the end of 1880 was based upon the separation of the Pará trade from the other Brazilian routes and the extension of the line to include the New York-Pará traffic.

The division of the trade in this way, not only acknowledged the growing importance of Pará, but also went some way towards recognizing the need for special types of ships for different kinds of cargo. The carriage of clean, high-value freight and of passengers was to be served by fast passenger-cargo liners, while the bulky, low-value goods, such as cotton and sugar, which characterized the trade of Ceará and Maranham, was to be transported in slower ships. An attempt was made to explore what has been called the 'essential economics of propulsion'—'that a ship of twice the capacity of another does not require double the horse power to propel it at the same speed'. The *Navigation* was chartered in January, 1880, and after loading coal at Cardiff, sailed to Havre, Lisbon and Pará, finally proceeding to New Orleans for cotton. The price of experience was a loss of £1,293. The North Brazilian trade was clearly not ready for the use of the 'weight carrying box', and Alfred Booth and Company found it impossible to compete with sailing ships which were able to carry coal to Brazil at 20s. a ton. In view of the size of the vessels employed as freighters by the end of the century, it is interesting to note that the Singlehursts were 'horrified' at the size of their new ship built in 1879, which was 1,830 gross tons. The use of the large cargo vessel in this trade was to be a later development,

E

even though the underlying principles of its use were recognized in 1880.

As the plan was envisaged, seven ships were required, two for the Pará route, and five others to maintain the slower service to the other ports. As a first step, the *Augustine* and the *Jerome* were placed at the end of 1880 on a fast monthly service to Pará and Lisbon, and the *Mirfield*, renamed the *Basil*, bought in October, 1880. The provision of so many additional ships was, however, beyond the scope of the older methods of finance, and it was agreed to convert the shipping interest into a joint stock company. The Booth Steamship Company Limited was in this way incorporated on June 24, 1881, with a nominal capital of £200,000 divided into £10 shares. £81,500 was issued in the first instance, largely to the existing partners in the original four ships and to other friends and the amount served to cover the assets of the old shipping interest and the purchase of the *Basil*.

The position of the shipping venture, as it stood in 1881, can be summarized thus: —

TABLE III

| Partner | | Number of sixty-fourth shares in | | |
	Augustine	Jerome	Ambrose	Bernard
Alfred Booth & Co.	49	49	20	33
Philip Holt ..	8	8	8	10
Alfred Holt ..	2	2	2	2
R. D. Holt ..	2	2	2	2
Hester Holt ..	2	2	2	2
James Quinn ..	1	1	—	—
Eills & Co. ..	—	—	4	4
Wm. Thornley ..	—	—	2	2
John Philips ..	—	—	—	1
T. B. Gunston ..	—	—	24	8
Value of ship	£14,080 0 0	£14,310 0 0	£16,975 0 0	£8,335 0 0
Reserve Fund	3,482 13 10	4,198 10 6	2,436 7 3	3,740 13 4
Total	17,562 13 10	18,508 10 6	19,411 7 3	12,075 13 4

£67,558 4s. 11d. was the value placed on the existing assets, of which £53,700 represented the four ships. Whether these figures were book or market valuations is not clear. If, however, these valuations are compared with the prices paid for the ships when built, they allow for an annual depreciation of between 2% and 2½% on the *Augustine, Jerome* and *Ambrose*. The reserve fund was clearly regarded as a deposit available to be drawn upon, up to the appropriate amount, by the individual partners. The amount invested by Alfred Booth and Company in the four ships was £40,350, and on the formation of the company the firm's holding was increased to £54,700. There was, also, approximately £56,000 of the partnership's capital in the leather side of the business at this time.

With the establishment of the new company, enquiries were made into the possibilities of the Pará-New York trade. The result of these was an arrangement by which, in return for an annual subsidy, a series of five voyages a year was provided from the up-river port of Manáos to New York, including a call at Pará. This was inaugurated in 1882, and was closely followed by a service to Antwerp and Hamburg to forestall opposition from a proposed German company and from the French Lines, Chargeurs Réunis and Compagnie Postale Transatlantique. To meet the needs of these new routes, the issued capital was raised to £125,000 and later to £141,450—again found from existing shareholders and friends—and with the extra money two ships were added to the fleet. These were the *Clement*, built in 1877, and the *Anselm*, a new vessel constructed by Leslie and Company, Newcastle-on-Tyne. This last vessel represented a bold departure, for cargo space was sacrificed in favour of passenger accommodation. Like the *Lanfranc*, built by T. Royden and Sons in 1882, it was a fast ship, with two propellers, designed expressly for the service from Liverpool to Pará. The final addition to complete the plan was also made in that year, when the *Cyril* was purchased. By January, 1885, the Booth Steamship Company had nine ships in commission with a total gross tonnage of 11,000. This expansion was paralleled by a similar growth in the tonnage operated by the Red Cross Line, with whom the Booth Steamship Company continued to work in close harmony. Both developments formed part of the rapid increase in the size of the steamship element in the British merchant marine, which rose from 4,449,000 gross tons in 1880 to 6,492,000 tons in 1885.

In the Booth Steamship Company the majority of the shares

continued to be held by Alfred Booth and Company, who remained the managers of the Line. For this work they received 10% of the net earnings of each ship, representing the sole administrative charges, other than the salary of the superintendent engineer. They shared with the Red Cross Line and the Maranham Steamship Company a berth in the Brunswick Dock, Liverpool, which they retained until 1902. For most of their shore servicing of ships, they depended upon the Ocean Steamship Company, whose owners, the Holts, were the largest shareholders other than the Booths.

In this way, after a period of stagnation for almost a decade, the growth of the shipping side of the business between 1880 and 1885 balanced the earlier expansion in the American leather trade. With the provision of a service from Manáos to New York, the shipping department there, which formerly dealt with vessels of other lines, was now more closely integrated into the structure of Alfred Booth and Company. And the import of goatskins from North Brazil, commenced in the 'eighties for the Gloversville factory, was soon to be matched by a regular export of American coal, flour and softwood to Pará and Manáos.

The business of Alfred Booth and Company, therefore, at the end of the 1880's, consisted of an export trade to America with a turnover of just over a quarter of a million pounds annually : a small tannery in Gloversville, which was profitable because of the application of 'dongola' tonnage to kangaroo skins : and the management of a fleet of nine ships, with a tonnage equivalent to that of two modern tramp steamers. It was a widespread rather than a large business. In London, at Fenchurch Street, Charles Booth had C. J. Garland and two other clerks; in Liverpool, where the offices had been moved from 5, India Buildings to 14, Castle Street in 1879, there were, apart from the partners, only a handful of men[2] By present-day standards, the hours of work were long, but the pace leisurely, far more so than in the American offices of the company. Another decade was to elapse before type-writing machines were introduced, and then in

[2] Of these A. E. Garland was particularly responsible for the work on the dockside, G. R. Heise, and later his son, F. G. Heise, for the accounts, John R. Webb was cashier, A. E. Mould superintendent engineer, and F. E. Miller was in charge of the freight department.

America first. Letters meanwhile continued to be written by hand and press copied into a book of tissue pages. To these Liverpool offices came Charles Booth once or twice weekly from London. There, standing for most of the day at a tall desk, he worked with concentrated energy, stopping only for a short luncheon of sandwiches and fruit. In America, there were eight persons in the main office in Broad Street, four at William Street, and three at Boston. Julius Kuttner managed the New York offices and A. E. Gaenslen that at Boston: both these men were to become partners in Alfred Booth and Company. Working with them were others who were to play a big part in the development of the business.

The period was a turning point in the growth of the business and in its administration. Henry Romilly returned from America a sick man and died in 1886; Alfred Booth was eager to retire, while neither of the remaining partners, Charles Booth and Thomas Fletcher, wished to make prolonged stays in New York. Thus from Autumn 1883 until the death of Julius Kuttner in 1902, there was no resident English partner in America; and by that date the second generation of the Booth family was ready to take its place in the firm. 'I want the business to be so organized,' wrote Charles Booth in 1883, 'here as well as in America that under superintendence and direction it goes of itself. This in order to have no more partners—and to give the excellent men who serve us a good future and to solidify the whole structure. Further I want the American side to be so perfect that it will run of itself with a yearly visit from this side. The immediate need for this is made by Romilly's illness. In England I should like it to be so that one of us, whether at Liverpool or London, could safely and without strain run the whole thing as I am doing by way of experiment at this moment. The active work of a second partner here, would then turn towards the working up of new business, which is essential to the life of any concern such as ours. Similarly the back and forth going of one or other of us between England and America would tend to keep breath in the body corporate and strengthen us where we are now weakest as compared with our opponents.' With the retirement of Alfred Booth in 1887, the plan was largely put into practice, Thomas Fletcher remaining the active Liverpool partner.

With the immediate problems of expansion in the leather and shipping sides of the business solved, at least temporarily, with the freedom from its day-to-day control granted him by the administrative changes initiated after 1883, Charles Booth was able to turn to his great social enquiries into the housing, wages, employment, health and religion of the people of London. The first fruits of these investigations appeared in the Journals of the Royal Statistical Society in 1886 and 1887, representing the application of those qualities of mind, which hitherto had been largely exercised in the world of commerce, to a new set of data.

CHAPTER V

The Surpass Leather Company
1890-1914

'The real plan of succeeding in business is to choose such a course that the tide of affairs is with you,' had been Charles Booth's dictum at the beginning of his career. Until the middle of the 'eighties the movement of this tide had been sluggish and the going correspondingly hard: for the next twenty-five years it was to flow strongly with the Booth interests. In 1885 the firm of Alfred Booth and Company had certainly not been a failure, but neither had it achieved outstanding success. When the War broke out in 1914, however, the Booth Steamship Company owned one of Liverpool's biggest lines and was a major element in the shipping trade to South America; at the same date, the other subsidiary, the Surpass Leather Company, had become an important unit in the American leather industry.

With Alfred Booth's withdrawal from active participation in the business, and the death of Thomas Fletcher in 1896, the period is closely associated with the leadership of Charles Booth. He was, at this stage in the company's history, 'tall, abnormally thin, garments hanging as if on pegs, the complexion of a consumptive girl, and the slight stoop of the sedentary worker, a prominent aquiline nose, with moustache and pointed beard barely hiding a noticeable Adam's apple, the whole countenance dominated by a fine-moulded brow and large, observant eyes . . . Observed by a stranger, he might have passed for a self-educated idealistic compositor or engineering draughtsman; or as the wayward member of an aristocratic family of the Auberon Herbert type; or as a university professor; or, clean-shaven with the appropriate collar, as an ascetic priest, Roman or Anglican; with another change of attire, he might have "made up" as an artist in the Quartier Latin. The one vocation which seemed ruled out alike by his appearance and by his idealistic temperament, was that of a great captain of industry pushing his way by sheer will-power and methodical industry, hardened and sharpened by an independent attitude towards other people's intentions and views—except as circumstances which had to be wisely handled—into new countries, new processes and new business connections. And yet this kind of adventurous and, as it turned out, successful profit-making enterprise proved his destiny, bringing in its train the personal power and free initiative due to a large income generously spent.'[1]

What is seldom, if ever, fully recognized is that Charles Booth's social investigations were carried out, not only by means of his share in the earnings of the company, but also when he was in active control of its affairs. It is, of course, true that in this aspect of his work, as in business, he had the help of a devoted band of assistants, of whom Beatrice Webb, his secretary—Jessie Argyle—Arthur Baxter, Ernest Aves, Sir Henry Llewellyn Smith, George Duckworth and Miss Clara Collet were some of the noteworthy members. Nevertheless, despite this help, and despite the existence of favourable business conditions, Charles Booth's dual success was a rare and great achievement.

In business, as in his social work, he was supported by an able group of colleagues. In all the major decisions advantage was taken of the mature judgment of his elder brother, Alfred Booth. It was fortunate, too, that from the middle of the 1890's onwards, the second generation of the Booth family were able to take an increasingly active share in the management of the company. After his second major breakdown in health in 1905-6, he was compelled to spend much of his time at Gracedieu Manor, Leicestershire, and the day-to-day control passed largely into their hands, although the firm's policy continued to be greatly influenced by him. Charles Booth (Junior), the eldest son of Alfred, became a partner in 1895, in which year his younger brother, Alfred Allen Booth (later Sir Alfred

---

[1] Beatrice Webb, *My Apprenticeship*, pp. 266-7.

Booth, Bt.) joined the company, as did George Macaulay Booth, the second son of Charles. They were later followed by Enfield and Tom Fletcher, sons of Thomas Fletcher. Following the example of their parents, the new generation took an active part in both sides of Alfred Booth and Company's activities, but, because of its growth, tended to specialize in either leather or shipping. G. M. Booth made the former his primary interest, and the sons of Alfred Booth the latter. With them were what might be called the first generation of 'Booth men'. In England, to mention a few, were the Garland brothers, J. R. Webb, F. G. Heise and Arthur Baxter: in Brazil, William Purcell, Benjamin Crimp, T. B. Southgate, Charles Good and J. Clissold: in the U.S.A., Julius Kuttner, Paul and David Crompton, C. H. Skinner and C. W. Jones (now Sir Clement Jones) and a host of others: in Australia, F. E. Miller. It was a strong team with an experienced captain.

The prosperity of these years rested on two developments; the discovery in America of a new system of tanning leather, and the fortunes of the Brazilian rubber industry. The adoption of chrome tannage represented 'the working up of new business which is', as Charles Booth wrote in 1883, 'the life of any concern such as ours'. This technical advance, which revolutionized the leather industry, was the discovery of an efficient method of tanning by chemical means, adaptable for hides and calfskins, but of particular value in producing a cheap kid leather. Its development in the decade 1890-1900, 'saw more progress in the art of leather manufacture than in any decade of the world'. The effect of the new technique was remarkable. While the consumption of hides in America between 1889 and 1899 increased 21%, and sheepskins 39%, that of goatskins multiplied 1600%. It now became possible to use kid leather in all the upper parts of footwear, where previously it had been confined to mere decoration and to the more expensive types of women's footwear. The production of this chemically tanned leather became the speciality of the Philadelphia district, the process spreading only slowly to other countries.

It is against this background that the expansion of the firm's leather interests must be understood. For the opportunities offered by this technical advance led not only to a growth, but also to re-orientation, of the business. In 1890, Alfred Booth and Company, with its New York counterpart, Booth and Company, were middlemen in pickled pelts, specializing in raw material for the Boston market, with a subsidiary interest in a small factory at Gloversville. Fifteen years later, this order of importance had been reversed. The manufacture of glazed and mat kid had now become the predominant activity, centred in a large factory in Philadelphia, with Gloversville as a subsidiary unit. In pickled pelts, the firm was still an important house, but the turnover in these goods represented only a quarter of that in kid leather. The centre of the leather business moved across the Atlantic, and the change was reflected in the re-appearance of resident English partners in New York. In the pickled pelt trade itself there were changes. The export of grains grew, while that of roans shrank, relatively and absolutely.

The decline in what had been the major element in the firm's leather business was due less to the diversion of capital into developing the new tannage than to increased competition from American sheepskin leather. The turning point can be dated from the collapse of the 'bastard' boom of 1893. Until then, with the exception of 1891, the years from the middle of the 'eighties had been profitable ones. An increasing population, the existence of generally prosperous conditions in America, the extension of machinery into the boot and shoe industry there, had all combined to produce a big demand for shoe leather. The problem in these years was that of finding an adequate supply of skins; this was the period when Alfred Booth and Company developed their New Zealand trade in pickled pelts and grain splits through the firm of Messrs. Bowron Brothers and established Mr F. E. Miller as their agent in Sydney. Originally sent out to obtain kangaroo and wallaby skins, which he bought at the Sydney auctions from dealers or directly from amateur and professional hunters, Mr Miller's field of activity was extended in 1894 to include the supervision of New Zealand sheepskin shipments from Christchurch. By the early years of the 1890's, some 6,000 casks containing 3,500,000 pickled pelts were annually sent by Alfred Booth and Company to America. Together with the shipments of grains, these pelts were distributed from three warehouses; in New York from 90, Gold Street, in Boston from 141, Purchase Street and 54, High Street, and from 126, 4th Street, Philadelphia.

The crisis of August, 1893, was followed by four years of depression in America, which were characterized not only by unemployment, but by war with Spain and by agitations over tariffs and currency. 'Capital does not feel safe in this country any more,' wrote Julius Kuttner from New York, 'the dollar of today may be a different one tomorrow. Sound money and peace would quickly make this country prosperous.' The Republican campaign for higher tariffs he regarded as the breeding ground for currency unrest; at bottom, according to him, it was 'a desire to punish foreigners and to give vent to hostile feelings against Europe and the world as a whole.' In these conditions, the impoverished farmers, disillusioned and further discouraged by the free importation of wool, diminished their flocks by two-fifths. As a consequence, the great firms of meat packers, particularly Swift and Company to whom these animals were sent for slaughter, became increasingly important in the sheepskin market. Selling for whatever price they could obtain for this by-product, they forced prices down to a minimum, which, though low, was not low enough to divert supplies to England. By January, 1896, stocks held by the company, on both sides of the Atlantic, amounted to £146,000, two and a half times greater than those held a year previously. The price of grains moved downwards in sympathy and for the greater part of 1894-6, the three English works—at Hitchin, Nuneaton and Lincoln—which supplied the American market, through Alfred Booth and Company, were closed. The resulting heavy losses in pickled pelts were borne, just as the increasing investment in kid leather manufacture was made possible, by the use of the greater part of the exceptional steamer profits of these years.

When economic activity revived in 1897, the amount of capital employed in kid leather exceeded that in pickled pelts. The importance of chrome tannage and increased supplies of American sheepskins made it abundantly clear that foreign roans would not again assume their former place in the structure of the business. The appearance of the meat packers in the leather trade and the progressive growth of the large tanners, with their own buying agencies abroad, narrowed the field for the independent middleman. The hegemony once exercised by Booth and Company over the Boston roan market was thus a thing of the past. It was symptomatic of the changed state of affairs that Boston sales for the first eight months of 1898 consisted of $300,000 worth of imported, and $200,000 of domestic sheepskins. Sales of American produced skins reached $430,900 in 1901 and continued to rise until 1907, when in the financial crash of that year the trade was temporarily abandoned. Although resumed later, it never again attained the same magnitude. The history of the Boston branch in the last years before the war can be summed up in the fact that while sales amounted to $1,143,778 in 1905, they had fallen to $359,048 six years later. In the other element of Alfred Booth and Company's exports to America—grain splits—the decline was slower. From 1894 to 1899, the losses on this type of skin had been heavy, but conditions improved with the turn of the century. The experience of the sheepskin business generally was that 'though lean years are more numerous than fat ones, still the fat ones, when they come, more than compensate for the lean ones.' With some 2,000 dozen skins weekly from the English factories, and between 2,000 and 3,000 weekly consigned either from England or New Zealand, a substantial business was maintained. In addition, there was a large sale of glue made by B. Cannon and Co., Ltd., Lincoln, in which tannery Alfred Booth and Company had acquired a substantial interest in the last years of the century. In 1901 the arrangements with the Nuneaton Leather Company were terminated and the Booths entered into partnership with Charles Wade, the tanner at Nuneaton, in the Whitemoor Works, Nottingham. Shortly afterwards the firm also withdrew from the Hitchin tannery, and concentrated its production of grains at Whitemoor and Lincoln. By 1910, the export of grains and foreign roans—the original but now subsidiary leather activity of the company— was grouped together under the title of Booth and Company (London) Ltd. with an office at 16, Railway Approach, London Bridge, where it was jointly managed by C. J. Garland and Arthur Baxter.

In the Gloversville factory, also, the depression of 1893-97 proved to be a turning point. The fall in the demand for expensive gloves made from kangaroo and horse hides, the infiltration of cheap kid into the glove business, and the development of leather and glove-making industries in the West exploiting local supplies of raw materials and local markets, had meant almost a decade of losses for the factory. In 1899 the range of its products was reduced to suede finished leather, mocha sheep castor, some gambier tanned leather, together with some fine shoe leather and kangaroo. Two years later the production of leather for glove making was abandoned altogether, and the plant was converted to the production of shoe leather, either in the form of kid or kangaroo.

The decline in the older aspects of the business was more than counter-balanced by the enormous expansion of Alfred Booth and Company's interest in the production of kid leather. In a very real sense the Gloversville factory was the parent of its own recession of prosperity. The making of kid leather by the 'tawing'[2] of goatskins, which Booth and Company obtained from Brazil, had long been one of its main functions. John Kent's discovery of the 'fatliquoring' process in 1878 and the development of 'Dongola' tannage had themselves been the result of constant efforts, in common with other American tanners, to find a cheap substitute for the expensive imported French kid, and for the laborious method of 'tawing'. 'Dongola' leather, particularly that made from kangaroo skins, had been extremely profitable. But while 'Dongola' leather proved fairly satisfactory for footwear, glazed 'Dongola' was less successful for more delicate work, where a softer material was required. For this reason, experiments continued, even after Kent's death in June 1886, with a view to making a good glazed alum leather. These proved to be both costly and unsuccessful; and Charles Booth turned to his cousin, Henry Roscoe, who suggested sending out a trained chemist from Owens' College, Manchester. The suggestion was not, however, implemented

---

[2] Tawing is a very old process of making leather, mainly from skins as distinct from hides. It consists in treating the skin with alum and salt, with the addition of an alkali such as sodium carbonate. The leather was finished by the application of egg yolk, dried, and then stored for six months.

because the factory was too small for so expensive a member of the staff. What is interesting, nevertheless, is that the experimental work at Gloversville led directly to the discovery of chrome tannage. This was the work of Augustus Schultz, a chemist employed by a New York firm of aniline dyers, who, by finding a way of making a permanent tannage with chrome salts, made the production of cheap kid leather possible. At the beginning of his experiments, Schultz 'knew no tanner in those days except Julius Kuttner, in the employ of Booth and Company, of Gloversville, N.Y. Mr Schultz asked Mr Kuttner if he knew of anything that would be an advantage to the leather trade, and he replied that it would be desirable to find something that would replace egg yolk which his firm were using for finishing their leather. Mr Schultz tried to find a substitute for egg yolk; but this experiment was a failure and Mr Schultz then commenced his experiments in tanning leather in 1880 and continued these experiments until his two patents were issued in 1844.'[3]

It is difficult to understand why the significance of the new method was not immediately recognized. The partnership letters, which are scanty for these years, are silent on the matter until 1889, when the patents had been sold to Messrs Blumenthal, an important Franco-American leather house. From this firm, they passed to Marcus Beebe and R. Foederer and Company, two of the leading Philadelphia leather dressers. It is probable that the process was initially regarded as just another in a series of successful and unsuccessful innovations which, at this time, were being applied to tanning. The merits of chrome tannage seem, however, to have gained increasing recognition in the early 'nineies, when the process was taken up by a number of Philadelphia tanners. With one of these, J. P. Mathieu, Booth and Company entered into an arrangement by which Brazilian goatskins supplied by them were chrome-tanned and glazed for a fixed dressing charge. The leather so made—a chrome-tanned, black, glazed kid—was marketed by Booth and Company under the name of 'Surpass'.

By 1894, chrome tannage had been introduced in a small way into the Gloversville factory both for goat and kangaroo

[3] C. T. Davis, *The Manufacture of Leather*, p. 327.

skins. At the same time, the output of 'Surpass' was growing fast and in 1896 involved a capital of £132,000. In that year, J. P. Mathieu extended his factory and the daily output of finished skins was pushed up to 600-700 dozen. In 1898 production was further increased to 1,000-1,200 daily; and the sales for the year amounted to 255,500 dozen skins—a daily average of 915—the receipts for which were $2,329,380 and the profit $109,979. Five years later, the output of the Philadelphia factory amounted to over 1,500 dozen skins daily, and the yearly sales of 'Surpass' to half a million dozen skins. Matthieu was a tanner of great ability, and from the beginning 'Surpass' leather took its place among the best of American manufactured kid; and this standing was enhanced by the company's selling methods. 'We keep even selections,' wrote Paul Crompton, 'and by being willing to make heavy losses sooner than alter this, and by our name and standing, create, and work on, a plane of our own.'

TABLE IV

Year	Sale price per doz. skins Leather $	Total output in dozen skins	Total sales in dozen skins
1898	9.12		255,500
1907	9.5	522,463	588,450
1908	9.05	477,362	564,518
1909	9.6	527,276	529,360
1910	9.86	587,495	599,037
1911	9.58	531,523	552,915
1912	9.74	499,896	569,006
1913	10.089	613,691	585,523

Linked with the development of glazed and mat kid leather in these early years, was a less successful venture in enamelled kid. This was the invention of George S. Wolff, another versatile chemist of German origin, by which it was hoped to supplant patent leather. It consisted of a fine, elastic and transparent lacquer, capable of being laid on leather so thinly that the natural beauty of its grain could be retained, as well as a high degree of softness and pliability. By an arrangement, made in 1898, it was agreed that some of the skins tanned at the Philadelphia factory should be enamelled by Wolff, and sold by Booth and Company under the trade name of 'Ideal'. When

Hanan and Wanamaker, and other footwear manufacturers, declared themselves in favour of the new leather, high hopes were entertained of its success. With the financial backing of Booth and Company, the Wolff Process Leather Company was formed and a large factory built at Summerdale on the outskirts of Philadelphia. But the leather did not live up to the expectations formed of it: largely because of the uneven quality of the lacquer, which frequently cracked and 'piped'. Wolff, himself, was more a man of promise than of achievement. 'For years and years, the man is in an experimental state,' grumbled the exasperated Julius Kuttner, 'will he go on for ever like this? Always blossoms, never any fruit.' The continued losses from the venture led inevitably to the withdrawal of Booth and Company from the Wolff Process Leather Company, and although the trade name 'Ideal' was retained, no further attempt was made to produce leather of this character after 1904.

Late in 1901, in the midst of this expansion of the American business, paralleled as it was in England by the formation of the second Booth Steamship Company, Julius Kuttner died, after nearly thirty years' service with the firm. With him went one of the few remaining links with the early days of Booth and Company. He had managed the New York house for over fifteen years, supported by frequent visits of the English partners and a constant correspondence with Charles Booth. When he assumed responsibility in 1884 the staff at New York and Boston numbered under twenty; at the time of his death they were nearly a hundred, divided into three departments, sheepskin, leather, and steamer and agencies.[4] The death of Julius Kuttner, although it did not stop the process of expansion, nevertheless created problems of management.

The responsibility for the American business devolved upon G.M. Booth, relieved from time to time by his cousin, A. A. Booth, and assisted by C. W. Jones, who joined the firm in 1902.

[4] The personnel in 88, Gold Street, New York, were: *Sheep Department*, J. F. Kaiser, manager, William Cunningham, salesman, David Roche, assistant salesman; *Steamer and Agencies Department*, Thomas Christie, manager and James Dinsmore, assistant manager; *Leather Department*, A. G. Grier, manager, H. H. Packer, Albert Millet and C. Heller salesmen, with Charles Missenharter as office manager. At Boston, A. C. Morrow was in charge of the sheepskin business and F. McClellan of the leather department. C. H. Skinner was factory manager at Gloversville.

But the simultaneous growth of other branches of the firm's activities, the increasing participation of A. A. Booth in the direction of the Cunard Line, and the double strain of business and social work which resulted in the collapse of Charles Booth in February, 1905, made it necessary for G. M. Booth to return to England. As a consequence, F. B. Kirkbride was appointed manager of the American interests in August, 1905. He resigned, however, in 1907, and was succeeded by Paul Crompton and C. W. Jones. The former, who had supervised the purchase of Chinese goatskins at Tientsin since 1902, became manager of the Surpass Factory, the latter taking charge of Booth and Company, New York, until 1910, when he returned to Liverpool as a director of the Booth Steamship Company; his place in New York being taken by Paul Crompton's brother, David.

These years also witnessed important changes in the relationship between the Philadelphia factory and Booth and Company. Until 1904, J. P. Mathieu and Company tanned, for a fixed charge, the skins supplied them by Booth and Company, who also marketed the finished leather. In December of that year, it was arranged that the profits of the manufacturing and sales organizations should be pooled and divided in accordance with an agreed scheme. This move towards integration was completed two years later when the Surpass Leather Company was formed, largely to control the quality and pace of production. The majority of the shares were then held by Booth and Company, with arrangements for the gradual liquidation of the holdings of J. P. Mathieu and Company.

The rapid growth of the tanning business between 1895 and 1905 brought a wide geographical extension of Alfred Booth and Company's interests, and with it a new range of problems. Foremost among these was the supply of goatskins. The abundance of this raw stock which since the 1850's had encouraged experiment, changed with the success of these experiments into relative scarcity. Surpass began as a speciality in Brazilian skins: by 1895 this source supplied only a third of its requirements, and attempts were being made to use Spanish and Levantine skins purchased from New York brokers, and fine Brazilian sheepskins called Cabrettas. Both proved unsatisfactory. The leather made from the first, sold under the name

F

of 'Eureka', was uneven in quality; while Cabrettas were soon imitated by cheaper leathers and thus became unattractive for expensive shoes. Booth and Company therefore turned to other areas, first to India and then to China. It was from these three areas—South America, India and China—that raw stock was drawn in the years before the Great War. India, in particular, was important; leather from Patna skins representing nearly half the output of the Philadelphia factory between 1900 and 1914.

The fact that the bulk of the world's goat population was (and is) tended by non-European peoples, meant the absence of highly developed collecting organizations. Like the many trickles of water which eventually unite into great rivers, travelling native hucksters collected skins from an infinite number of settlements, bringing them to urban dealers in noisy bazaars and dusty market places. These dealers roughly sorted them into various categories and sold, or transferred, them to merchants at the ports, who in turn brought them into the stream of international trade. And the direction of the stream before the great war was towards the U.S.A., where 80% of the 100-120 million goatskins in international trade was absorbed. This wide dispersion of supply and its necessary combination with dealings in other types of skins and hides, together with the size of Surpass requirements, led Booth and Company to depend upon the merchants in their main supply centres, rather than buy themselves, as with kangaroo skins, or depend upon importing brokers in New York. Many of these merchants were old-established Jewish houses of considerable importance. Hess and Hirsh supplied skins collected at Pernambuco: Rossbach and Delmiro those from Ceará, Pará and Bahia: and Cohn Brothers and Fuchs, whose headquarters were at Zurich, those collected at Calcutta. In China, the buyers were Liddell Brothers, one of the great English merchant houses in that country. The importance of the Indian supplies to Surpass led to a close collaboration between itself and Cohn Brothers and Fuchs. This was made the more necessary because of the great variations in goatskins. For there is not only a range of sizes and weights of skins (with important consequences on the cost of tanning), but the quality of the finished leather is profoundly affected by the character of the animal's environment, the age at which it is slaughtered and the method by which the skin is cured. And in no continent are there wider divergences than in India. As a result, Cohn Brothers and Fuchs received precise instructions with regard to the assorting of skins. Amritsar skins, for example, were separated into those which came from hill-bred and from plain-bred animals: the latter were divided into skins from well-watered areas and from desert areas: and all were subject to a size distinction. This assortment, further refined at Philadelphia, was of immense importance in the production of a high-grade, uniform product, and was a basic factor in the success of Surpass leather.

During the ten years which preceded the Great War, the Surpass Leather Company produced about an eighth of the 240 million square feet of kid leather annually manufactured in the U.S.A. The quantities of skins drawn from the markets of the world were thus very considerable; and, as the cost of skins represented about six-tenths of the value of finished leather, this part of the business was of great significance. The buying season in India and China—to a lesser extent in South America —was from September to April: and once the long chains of middlemen were set in motion, it took almost three months to halt them. The buying programme was thus formulated in advance; generally, in the middle of the year, and was based on the prices of leather and the quantities sold in June to September, the doldrums of the American market. The long period between the buying of the skin and its appearance in the warehouse as finished leather—about four months—was bridged with the aid of financial assistance from the banks, whose function it was to facilitate this step in the process of production.

The construction of the buying programme, with its need for accurate forecasting, formed part of the general policy of 'free selling', or the avoidance of stocks, which governed the conduct of Surpass Leather Company in these years. With his innate love of system, Charles Booth laid down an ideal, which was to maintain a stock of skins, either waiting or in process of production, equivalent to 75 days' output, and of finished leather equal to 45 days average sales. In actual practice, of

course, there were fluctuations around this norm. This programme in itself, however, involved anything between
£400,000 and £500,000 of capital. It is thus easy to see why
'free selling' was insisted upon. Not only did it avoid the
accumulation of large amounts of stagnant capital, but there
were also considerable advantages to be gained from keeping a
large factory working at full capacity. Further, the inelastic
character of skin supplies made raw stock prices fluctuate more
widely than those for finished leather, so that, within limits,
the smaller the stocks the greater the gains from a market so
constructed. Only once was this policy abandoned. In 1906, the
upward trend of prosperity in America led Booth and Company to buy large amounts of skins, thus forcing raw stock
prices upwards. Sales of leather were reduced in order to bring
its value into line with that of raw stock, thus reversing the
natural relationship. As a consequence, there was a sharp rise
in the stock of skins, and a lesser one in finished leather. By
January, 1907, these amounted to over three million dollars,
sustained by a loan of £300,000 from Alfred Booth and Company and one of nearly £400,000 from Baring Brothers. The
liquidation of these stocks after June, 1907, involved substantial losses, and for nearly a year the Surpass Leather Company
dominated the American kid leather market and consequently
those for raw stock. But when the financial crisis of the autumn
of 1907 affected the American economy, the Surpass factory
was the only one in Philadelphia able to pay its workmen in
cash.

With customary lucidity, Charles Booth summed up the
lessons of this experience, in one of his last long business
memoranda.

'1. The smaller the capital employed in conducting a business
    of fixed volume, the larger the possible ratio of profit.
2. The more rapidly raw stock, once purchased, is converted
    into cash, the smaller will the capital involved be.
3. From these two principles it is evident that prompt sales
    increase the possibility of profit.
4. One of the most important parts of the leather business is
    the lowest price to pay for raw material. To know this it is
    necessary to make an experiment in raw material and to

understand thoroughly the material you have purchased. The material must be manufactured and sold and complete confidence given to the skill in both departments. After this it is justifiable to make further purchases in accordance with the result of your experiment. Practically speaking, the general course of your business must, to some extent, follow the stricter course indicated above for fresh experiment, that is to say, no permanent buying methods can be satisfactory unless your purchases are intended to replace the material which was used to make the finished product you have just been selling. Of all manufacturing business, that dealing with skins most requires to be a constant stream and no theoretic or speculative ventures have any right to exist.

5. As a maxim on selling, it can be truly said that no one needs more experience or more constant training. To Americanize, it is essential for buyer and seller to get the habit of dealing with each other. Fine offices and highly-paid salesmen make it necessary to get higher prices for our leather, but do not of themselves sell it, and it may here also be added that insensate over-capitalization hampers still further the work of a salesman by increasing the price he has to try to get. The only possible way of standing the expenses of an expensive sales organization is to spread that expense over an enormous volume of sales. Let it be understood that the margin of possible profit is very limited. A very little carelessness in buying, or in manufacturing, will eliminate it, and strictest economy in the finance department and a wide sense of proportion between selling expenses are essential to the discovery of any profit margin at all at the close of the year's trading.'

But the geographical extension of Alfred Booth and Company's business interests was affected not only by the areas from which it drew the raw material for Surpass, but also by the centres from which the finished product was distributed. In addition to the warehouses in New York and Boston—at 90, Gold Street and 39, South Street respectively, in 1910—the development of the boot and shoe industry in the middle west and in the southern states saw the extension of the sales organization into these areas. In 1902, G. M. Booth visited St Louis, which he found 'bursting with vitality', and, as a consequence of his visit, opened a branch at 701, Lucas Avenue. This was followed in quick succession by branches at 801/3, Sycamore Street, Cincinnati, and at 20, Andrew Street, Rochester. From these centres, salesmen, equipped with motor-cars in 1914, visited local factories. But perhaps the most interesting feature was the growth of an export trade to Europe, where chrome tannage, with the exception of a small industry in Germany, had hardly made an appearance. In this, Booth and Company had been anticipated by other manufacturers, who found in this outlet a useful counter-balance to the seasonal nature of the American market. In England, Lilley and Skinner were the first to make use of Surpass leather, and in 1899 the overseas sales amounted to 20,165 dozen out of a total sale of 317,150 dozen skins. By the end of this year, however, a kid leather warehouse was established at 50, St Thomas's Street, Bermondsey, and a small staff engaged under Alec Little. By 1903, the sales in England amounted to £75,000 and five years later to £220,000. For the same year, 1908, the value of pickled pelts sold in the old-established Boston store at 141, Purchase Street, was £350,000. Parallel with the growth of the English market was the development of that in Europe. Since 1899 a good deal of Surpass leather had found its way to France and Germany through Lowenstein and Company, New York, and in 1904 they became its recognized distributors in these countries. Further arrangements were made in the following years for sales to other countries, and a substantial trade grew up with Russia. In this way, the diminishing volume of sheep-skins moving westwards across the Atlantic was balanced by a growing eastward movement of finished goatskin leather.

After the losses incurred in 1907, came two years of prosperity, followed in 1910 by another bad year, and then a revival of prosperity, which lasted for the remaining years of peace, despite labour troubles in Philadelphia in 1911 and 1912. The most important development of these years was the attention directed towards the by-products of the factories at Gloversville and Philadelphia—the trimmings of skins used in making glue and the hair employed in the manufacture of felt.

With a total yearly consumption of 500,000-600,000 dozen skins, the quantities involved were large; and in 1912 the revenue thus derived from the trimmings and hair amounted to $127,329, or the equivalent of the dividend on Surpass Preference Shares. The natural and inevitable consequence was to seek a stable market for these products. Accordingly, in 1912 and 1913, interests were acquired in two American concerns, the Gardiner-Lucas Glue and Gelatine Corporation and the Densten Felt and Hair Company.

By 1914, therefore, a great change had occurred both in the size and the character of the American leather business. The central feature was now the Surpass Leather Company, with its headquarters located in the offices of Booth and Company, New York, and its allied concerns in glue and felt. Quantities of sheepskins were consigned to America, but it was a much diminished activity. Almost as important were the exports of English glue from the Lincoln factory, which found a ready sale across the Atlantic. Twenty years earlier, Booth and Company had been predominantly merchants, now they were largely manufacturers. And the problems of acquiring raw materials and the distribution of leather brought the firm into touch with all parts of the world. Side by side with this expansion went the growth of the shipping business, which also had important repercussions on the shipping department of Booth and Company, New York. In 1914, 27% of the tonnage of the Booth Fleet was employed between American ports, and half the distance traversed by the ships was in American waters.

CHAPTER VI

The Booth Steamship Company
1881-1914

The remarkable expansion of the older branch of Alfred Booth and Company's activities during the period 1890-1914 was balanced by an equally rapid growth of its shipping interest. In the same way that the Surpass Leather Company became an important element in the American leather industry, so also did the Booth Steamship Company in the shipping trade of Liverpool. And as both developed into independent units. the functions of the mother company became more and more those of a holding and financing organization.

The founding of the first Booth Steamship Company in 1881 was marked by a revival of French competition, and for nearly two years the Chargeurs Réunis struggled unsuccessfully to obtain a foothold in the North Brazilian trade. The conflict was fought to maintain a dominant position in a trade which was both small and specialized; and the history of the next thirty years is the story of the successful maintenance of this position. The immediate effect of the struggle, however, together with the generally depressed state of English trade, was to make the years 1883 to 1885 singularly unprosperous ones. For Alfred Booth and Company the situation was to some extent mitigated by the success of 'Dongola' tannage in America; but for the steamship company itself, with no dividends in 1883-5, it was an inauspicious beginning. Yet despite adverse conditions, the struggle with Chargeurs Réunis led in these years to two tactically important, if initially unprofitable, extensions—the services run to include Antwerp and Hamburg and that between Manáos and New York. Both were designed to prevent steamship lines from gaining an entry into the trade, from which more prosperous routes could be attacked. After the decision to call at Oporto in 1888, for which the *Laurinium*, re-named *Gregory*, was purchased, seven years were to pass before any further modification was made in the services provided by the Booth and Red Cross Lines.

These were years of steady although not spectacular progress. Prosperity returned to the North Brazilian trade in 1886, and from 1888 onwards the years were 'golden'. In 1885, there were nine ships amounting to 11,000 gross tons; at the beginning of 1895 there were eleven ships, whose gross tonnage was over 17,000. The four original boats were sold and replaced by six larger ones. The *Ponca* was bought in 1890; the *Gloamin* (renamed the *Origen*) in 1891; and the *Red Sea* (renamed the *Hilary*) in 1892. In addition, two intermediate liners were constructed by Hall, Russell and Company, Aberdeen: the *Hildebrand* in 1893 and the *Hubert* in the following year. Not only were the ships, on average, as large as that which horrified the Singlehursts fifteen years earlier, but their average age had been considerably reduced. Despite this development, the Booth Line remained only a small unit in the structure of Liverpool shipping: the Holts, for example, had a gross tonnage of 72,622 in 1895, the Lamport and Holt Line 92,614 and the Cunard 85,596.

Excluding the direct Maranham-Liverpool sailings made by the Maranham Steamship Company, the Amazon trade was accommodated by four services at the beginning of the 'nineties. There was the fast and predominantly passenger route to Pará, via Lisbon and Oporto, on which the Booth Line had two, and the Red Cross Line, three ships. This was generally the most prosperous series of voyages; in 1886—a year of recovering trade—the gross receipts earned on twelve voyages were £32,642 for freight and £18,165 for passenger transport. Secondly, there was the new Continental route via Hamburg, Antwerp, Havre and Lisbon to the Brazilian ports, a service often profitable in summer only. On this, each company had three ships. Thirdly, there was a joint monthly service to Ceará and Maranham via Lisbon and Oporto; and finally the subsidized voyages between Manáos and New York. This last was worked in with the Maranham and Ceará sailing to avoid the expense of a large shipping department at New York.

Although increased exports from Brazil of coffee, maté, cocoa, nuts and skins swelled the flow of goods, it was upon rubber that the growing prosperity of the 'River' depended. The sap of the wild hevea tree had been collected for commercial use for nearly forty years, during which the output from North Brazil had risen from 31 tons in 1822 to 8,679 tons in 1880. It was, however, with the invention of the pneumatic tyre in 1888, and the subsequent development of bicycles and motor vehicles, that the demand for rubber grew apace. In the 'eighties, the production of Brazilian rubber doubled to reach 16,394 tons in 1890; by 1900, it had further increased to 27,650 tons and reached a peak of 44,296 tons eleven years later. And although by this date the growing output of plantation rubber was piling up sombre clouds on the horizon of Amazonian prosperity, Brazil still accounted for 46% of world production. As demand stiffened, the price of rubber moved upwards. 'In the late 'seventies the average price of all rubber imported (into England) was 1s. 1d. a lb.; in 1901-5 it was 2s. 6d.: in 1909-13 it was 3s. 8½d.'[1] Under this impetus the economic activity of the Amazon blossomed with tropical exuberance. Prosperity led to large public and private building of all kinds, financed partly by the wealth of the 'rubber barons', partly by English, French, Belgian and American capital. Harbours were built at Pará and Manáos and at Iquitos in Peru; and there was further development of river settlements, such as Obidos, Santarém and Itacoatiara. There were electricity and gas installations, tramways and public improvements. Manáos, the centre of the rubber trade, 'had an electric line before Liverpool. She installed telegraph, telephone, and adequate sewerage. She became, and still is, one of the cleanest cities of the world. Fine public buildings were erected'.[2] The Opera House, Teatro do Amazonas, prefabricated in England, was erected at a cost of £2 million, and its magnificence was equalled in some of the mansions of the rubber magnates. In addition to all this, there were the railways, of which the Madeira-Mamoré line, linking the Madeira river and its Bolivian extension, was perhaps the grimmest

[1] J. H. Clapham, *An Economic History of Modern Britain*, Vol. III, p. 143.
[2] Willard Price, *The Amazing Amazon*, p. 151.

venture. For this 'railroad of the dead', as it has been called, the Booth Steamship Company carried labourers from Lisbon and Oporto to Itacoatiara, at the junction of the Madeira and Amazon rivers for £6 10s. a person and railway iron from America at 30s. a ton. The inward flow of immigrants, the carriage of bulky cargoes and the frequent visits of wealthy Brazilians to Europe all rested on the outward movement of rubber. These factors can be seen in the value of exports and imports of the states served by the ports at which the English steamships called:—

TABLE V

	Exports			Imports		
	1886	1895	1905	1886	1895	1905
River States						
Amazonas	5.15	44.84	109.40	1.91	4.34	19.45
Pará	29.11	47.44	106.52	9.58	26.92	44.98
Coastal States						
Ceará	6.50	1.90	8.50	5.79	4.75	5.92
Maranham	5.57	4.00	7.63	6.92	4.74	9.27

(Figures quoted in millions of reis)

The control over the lifting of this enormously increased traffic was effected in three broad ways: by the provision of adequate tonnage, by the creation of loading and discharging facilities at the various ports and by a reasonable policy adopted with regard to freight rates.

Because the high rate of immigration into Brazil spelt 'golden years' for the two lines between 1888 and 1894, the early stages of this increased outward shipment of bulky cargoes was allowed to slip past the Liverpool companies. It was not until the prosperous year of 1895, that the large volume of cargo, coinciding with a renewed passenger traffic, caused alarm. 'So long as we could take the cream and leave the skim milk,' wrote Charles Booth, 'it was nice business, but it could not possibly last. There is stone for paving Manáos, and building stone for Pará from Lisbon and Oporto, there is also coal for the Amazon Company at Manáos, and possibly at Pará too—there has been bridge work for Manáos, and electric plant for Pará and railway iron for tramways and there has been a quantity of lighters sent out in sections. All these things are going and will continue to go, being a natural consequence of the prosperity of the Amazon

Valley. In addition the rather high level of freight tariff has brought sailing vessels into the field. Large importers who order enough to make up the bulk of a cargo instruct their friends to put up a sailing ship, and lots of cargo has been taken from us in this way, at Hamburg and Oporto, at Lisbon as well as at New York. So long as this was confined to sailing ships and we could fill our ships at full rates, this did not much matter, but when these part cargoes were made the excuse for putting on a steamer, combined with stone or coal, we were obliged to fight. We have let this thing go on too long so that the brokers who have taken it up talked of regular monthly departures for the next two years.' If the extension of the fleet in 1881 was the second turning point in the history of the Booths' shipping interest, the decision to carry bulky cargo with all that it implied —a decision implicit in Charles Booth's words—must be regarded as the third.

It represented the fulfilment of the experiment carried out with the *Navigation* in 1880, but now in conditions which made the employment of a 'weight carrying box' an economic possibility. Taking advantage of the low building costs in 1895, and with aid provided by the Bank of Liverpool, two large vessels were ordered from Barclay, Curle and Company, Glasgow—the *Dominic* and *Dunstan*, each of 2,966 gross tons; in the same year the *Horsley Towers*, a ship of similar tonnage, was purchased from Messrs T. Wilson and Sons. In 1896, the *Polycarp*, a sister of the *Dominic* and *Dunstan*, was launched, and the *Grantully Castle* (renamed *Augustine*) was acquired from D. Currie and Company. The following year saw the purchase of the *Leyden* (renamed *Benedict*) and the *Warwick Castle* (renamed *Jerome*); in 1898, the *Mourne* (renamed *Basil*) and the *Mount Sirion* (renamed *Bernard*). Thereafter, for the next two years, the pace slackened. Only the *Cresswell* (*Gregory*) was added to the fleet in 1899 and the *La Plata* (*Clement*) in 1900. Thus in five years, the character of the fleet had changed. After the sale of the smaller vessels, there were in 1900 fourteen ships as compared with eleven in the early part of 1895. But the gross tonnage had more than doubled and the average net tonnage of the individual ships—other than smaller and faster vessels, the *Hilary*, *Hildebrand* and *Hubert*—

increased from 1,043 to approximately 2,000 tons.

Because the homeward freight from the Amazon was small in bulk, and the heavy outward cargoes for development purposes irregular in occurrence, the efficient handling of these larger ships involved two important problems. The first was surmounted by sending the ships in ballast from Pará to Galveston, on the Gulf of Mexico, for cotton, and, occasionally, grain shipments. Thus the largest boats made a triangular voyage: out to Brazil, with coal and rough cargo, and then to Galveston, and home to Liverpool. On this route, the profit of the voyage depended largely on the freight rates obtained on the last stage of the journey from Galveston to Liverpool. Secondly, the regular outward employment of ships was obtained by carrying coal from England for the bunkering of ships abroad, for use by river steamers, and for gas and electricity plants in the Amazon valley. It had been unprofitable to carry coal to Pará in 1880 for 20s. a ton, but in 1900 this was performed for 15s. 6d. and to Manáos—900 miles up river—for 18s. 6d. In 1911, these rates were, respectively, 13s. and 18s., and to Iquitos, some 6,100 miles from Liverpool, 40s. a ton. In that year, coal f.o.b. Cardiff at 15s. 3d. a ton was delivered at Pará for 38s. (including port duties and discharging expenses), Manáos 42s. 11d. and Iquitos 68s. a ton. In times of heavy outward shipments of ordinary cargo, coal was carried in chartered vessels: in this way providing an elasticity of tonnage, as well as enabling the company to build when costs were low. 'The value of handling and maintaining a regular hold on the coal trade, if it can be so worked as to justify larger ships or more frequent departures, and full loads every time, is very important and is profitable whatever the freight rates may be that tramps or sailing vessels may offer. This policy we have successfully pursued,' explained Charles Booth in 1915, 'it presupposes an average of space over and above the requirements of other cargo, and gives the elasticity needed to even up differences in capacities of liners employed and seasonal and other variations in volume of ordinary trade. It demands friendly relations and consideration for the interests of shippers of coal on a give and take basis. Whether the freight may be 3d. more or 3d. less than others would accept is immaterial.

The advantage offered is a steady stream of supplies which obviates carrying of large stocks and minimises the risk and uncertainties of delivery, and if never taken undue advantage of, establishes a habit and connection of great value. It may lead to our supplying the coal by increasing our own contracts, or chartering the tonnage, if charters are needed, and in every other way tends to put us firmly in the saddle against any liner competition.'

Side by side with this rapid expansion of tonnage to meet the requirements of trade went two other major developments. In 1897, four of the older boats—the *Cyril, Basil, Clement*, and *Gregory*—displaced by the larger ones built or bought in the preceding two years, were on the suggestion of Charles Booth, employed on the Brazilian coast under the Brazilian flag. A syndicate was formed to run this service, named the Empreza Line, in which the Booth Steamship Company held a quarter share. These ships, with the *Grenville*, obtained in 1897, were under the management of the Pará agent (first William Purcell and, on his death, Captain Crimp) returning to Liverpool periodically for overhaul. As an investment for part of the steamship company's reserves, the Empreza Line proved a profitable venture, but disagreement with the Brazilian merchants, who held three-quarters of the shares of the line, led to the withdrawal of the Booth interest in 1901. The second development was the formation of the Booth Iquitos Steamship Company to compete with that set up by the Red Cross Line. Of the £50,000 capital, the Booth Steamship Company held just over half, the remainder being contributed by the Amazon River Steam Navigation Company and by merchants in Iquitos and Pará, among whom Charles Ahrenfeldt and F. Wesche were the most important. The service was inaugurated by the *Clement*, commanded by Captain John Jackson, who came out of retirement for the purpose. The vessel left Liverpool at the end of March, and after an uneventful voyage arrived at Iquitos on May 24, 1897. In the following year, two small ships, the *Huascar*, and the *Bolivar* were acquired specially for the direct Liverpool-Iquitos run, and made their maiden voyages in that year, a round journey of 12,800 miles. This, too, proved a profitable venture, for the *Huascar*, which cost £15,000 to build, made

£10,000 profit on her first three voyages. Later a direct service between New York and Iquitos was also established. Finally, the alliance between the company and the Amazon River Steam Navigation company was cemented by the acquisition of a substantial holding in the latter concern.

Although the tonnage of the Booth Steamship Company had thus doubled since 1895, the pace of Brazilian development was such that, by the end of the century, it bid fair to outstrip the carrying capacity of the two Liverpool lines. The position was, however, complicated by the fact that the Red Cross Line had not adapted its ships to carry the growing volume of bulky cargo, and, secondly, by the imminent retirement of the senior partners of R. Singlehurst and Company, the biggest shareholders of that line. In a period of active steamship amalgamations, the danger lay in the possibility that the Red Cross Line might be acquired by one of the larger companies. The Hamburg-America Line, under the control of the remarkable Albert Ballin, had already edged into the Amazon trade, and showed every sign of a desire to obtain a larger share; his expansionist policy having been recently demonstrated by the enormous sum paid for the good will of an Italian steamship line sailing to the River Plate. In Liverpool itself there was considerable activity of the same kind. The Leyland Line, then the largest fleet based on the port, had in fact approached the Singlehursts in 1897 with a view to buying their ships, and had since purchased the West Indian and Pacific Line. Three years later, it was itself to be absorbed into the great shipping combine headed by Pierpont Morgan, the American financier. There was also the possibility that the rapidly growing Elder Dempster Line might wish to extend its interests southwards to the Amazon. 'More than likely,' observed Charles Booth, 'any of these would end in our absorption on some terms or another into a big concern—or being clean bought out. We might do very well as to money, I dare say. In fact, I think we should manage to hold our own one way or another, but our nice private business would be gone.'

From the point of view of Alfred Booth and Company, already under considerable financial strain because of the simultaneous expansion of both its major interests, there was little chance of buying out the Singlehursts. In these circumstances, the situation narrowed itself down to an amalgamation of the two lines under the control of the Booth family, but with safeguards for the capital of the Singlehurst family. On this basis, negotiations were opened in 1900 and slowly proceeded into the early months of the following year. In the midst of them, on January 21, 1901, 'Our great Queen died and it is hard to think of anything else', wrote one of the younger Booths to Julius Kuttner. 'The whole balance of the world is thrown off its centre and has to right itself gradually.' Two months later, however, the difficulties between the two concerns were finally settled and the Booth Steamship Company (1901) Ltd. was registered. The new venture had a capital of £550,000, divided into 30,000 5½% cumulative preference shares and 25,000 ordinary shares, each of £10. An attempt was made to float a 5½% first mortgage debenture stock to the value of £450,000, but this proved a failure—'newspapers in which we refused to advertise went for the issue'—and only £100,000 was obtained, nearly half of which represented money already on deposit with the company. In the event, the Singlehursts received £300,000 in debentures and £70,000 in preference shares, together with two places on the board of directors. The shareholders of the old Booth Steamship Company obtained three preference shares for each £10 ordinary share formerly held. The combined fleets represented 65,000 gross tons and the way was clear for a further expansion of the business.

Under the continued development of the Amazon valley, the gross tonnage of the new Booth Steamship Company doubled itself again between 1901 and the outbreak of the Great War, reaching a peak of 125,603 tons in 1910, excluding the 3,500 tons of its subsidiary, the Iquitos Steamship Company. This was a substantial achievement; but the full measure of the change can best be seen when the figures for 1910 are compared with those of the early months of 1895. Such a comparison reveals a fourfold increase in Liverpool shipping engaged in the Amazon trade. How extraordinary this growth was, in relation to the general state of British and foreign shipping, is reflected in the indices of estimated steamship deadweight carrying capacity compiled by the Liverpool Shipowners' Association:[3]

Year	U.K.	Other Countries	World
1895	100	100	100
1900	123	150	134
1906	169	220	191

Some additions to the fleet were made in most years, but 1904-6 and 1910, when ship-building costs were low, were outstanding for the amount of construction ordered.

One important advantage of the amalgamation of the two lines was the opportunity provided for the building of special types of vessels. The major expression of this was the construction of ships designed for passenger transport after the sharp increase in homeward traffic which began in the Spring of 1902. The *Madeirense*, which sailed from Pará in May of that year, for example, carried fifty extra first-class passengers over its normal complement, with similar overcrowding in the third-class accommodation. The immediate position was met by the purchase of the *Hawarden Castle* (*Cyril*) which made her first voyage to the Amazon in November 1902. Thereafter the company embarked upon a considerable programme of passenger liner building. The *Ambrose* was ordered from Raylton Dixon & Company, and was delivered in October 1903. The *Anselm* was built at Belfast in 1904, at a prime cost of £89,000. In October of the following year, two larger, twin-screw, ships of the same kind were ordered: the *Lanfranc*, 6,275 gross tons, from the Caledon Shipping and Engineering Company, Dundee, for £122,000, and the *Antony*, from Hawthorn Leslie & Company for £123,000. The *Hilary*, a sister ship of the *Lanfranc*, was added to the fleet in 1909; and the *Hildebrand* in 1911. There was also the *Vincent*, a shallow draught vessel of 915 gross tons, built in 1909 with a view to navigating the Rio Madeira to tap the possible development of the Bolivian trade after the completion of the Madeira-Mamoré Railway.

The organization of this increased tonnage into the various routes altered surprisingly little between 1897, when the ships first went to Galveston, and the outbreak of war in 1914. In-

---

[3] *Annual Report of the Liverpool Shipowners' Association*, 1910.

G

creased passenger traffic meant calls at additional ports in Europe, and the development of North Brazil brought new ones into existence there. But for most of the period, there was little change within the rough quadrilateral composed of New York, the Amazon, Liverpool and the west European ports. In 1902, calls at Antwerp, Rotterdam and Hamburg, except for the Iquitos trade, were abandoned under a pooling arrangement with the Hamburg-America Line, while in the same year the Maranham and Parnahyba trade was acquired when Hugh Evans and Company were bought out. Basically, the service consisted of a monthly sailing to Manáos via Plymouth, Cherbourg, Vigo, Oporto, Lisbon, Madeira and Pará, thence home by the same route: the 'C' line of large cargo vessels, which after loading coal at Cardiff went out direct to Pará and Manáos, thence to Galveston and home to Liverpool: a 'D' line which after calling at Cardiff, sailed to North Brazil and then direct to England: finally, two lines, later combined, one of which called at the continental and coast ports of North Brazil, and a second which carried passengers and cargo between New York and the Amazon. The two Iquitos companies were merged in 1901 and eleven years later absorbed into the parent company. Their ships went out via Cardiff, Havre, Hamburg, Lisbon, Pará and Manáos to Iquitos, thence to New York and back to Iquitos, returning home after calling at Lisbon and Havre.

There were only two major extensions of the services provided by the Booth Steamship Company during these years. The first was the establishment of tours to Lisbon and Madeira in 1903. The development of a regular service of fine passenger vessels leaving Liverpool on, or about, the 10th, 20th and 30th of each month for Manáos, with equally regular arrival dates at Liverpool, enabled the company to make such arrangements. The tours proved extremely popular and hundreds of passengers were carried each year in this way. Secondly, the possibility of entering the frozen meat trade had been explored in 1902, but unsettled financial conditions in England, the poor trade of that year in the Amazon valley, together with German competition, led to an indefinite postponement of the plan. In the circumstances, Charles Booth had written, 'I don't mind some shrinkage of the business—even if it lasted for a year or so—it has been growing too fast for both our capital and our capacity of management.' It was not again considered until 1910, when it was not the frozen meat, but the general cargo trade, which the company had in view, as well as the strengthening of its position against possible competition from the Hamburg-America Line. Negotiations were begun for four boats —then building for the Elder Dempster Line. Only one of these proved suitable, later called the *Christopher*—and three others were ordered from R. & W. Hawthorn, Leslie and Company, at a cost of £198,000. The service was commenced in 1911, and the four ships sailed direct to Buenos Aires after loading coal at Cardiff, thence to New York, calling at the larger North Brazilian ports, and then returning to Pará, northwards again to Galveston and then, loaded with cotton, crossed the Atlantic to Liverpool. Largely a tactical move, the service was run only at a very considerable cost.

The second group of factors in the successful maintenance of the Amazon shipping business—the provision of adequate loading and discharging facilities at the North Brazilian ports— grew side-by-side with the expansion in tonnage. Within a decade of the founding of the line, lack of adequate harbour installations had led to the provision of lighters and hulks at Ceará, Maranham and Pará. In 1879, the senior captain, Captain John Jackson, suggested the provision of a lightship at Pará. 'They have wanted a lightship in Pará for more than a year,' he wrote. 'The Imperial Government will not decide about it and the President had to pay for the schooner he bought as a temporary lightship.' With the development of Amazon trade the need for these facilities increased, and together with the unsatisfactory character of some of the Brazilian agents, led to the establishment of the company's own agencies in Pará and Manáos in 1886. These were followed by houses in Iquitos in 1903 and in Maranham, Parnahybá and Ceará in 1912-13. When the amalgamation of the two lines took place in 1901, there were in North Brazil 78 lighters, some of them capable of carrying 200 tons; thirteen years later, local facilities for handling cargo included 134 lighters, 16 tugs, and 7 pontoons.

The most important development of this kind, however, was the establishment of the Manáos Harbour in 1902. This originated in a concession granted to Baron Rymkiewics, a Polish nobleman, and to Mr Lavandeyra, an able Cuban engineer, who, with the support of the firm, founded the Manáos Harbour Ltd. Alfred Booth and Company had thus from the first a substantial and, for a period, a controlling interest in the project. The installations, consisting of a series of large pontoons which rose and fell some fifty feet with high and low water, and a series of large warehouses, were formally opened in May, 1903. Work continued for several years thereafter and by June, 1907, almost £750,000 had been spent on harbour works. In February, 1904, a muelle, or wharf, was opened at Iquitos for the use of the company's ships: this never in itself proved profitable, although of considerable advantage to the ships loading and discharging there. Both establishments were of great significance in determining the attitude of the company towards the Amazon river, for they committed it to a policy of up-river development instead of concentrating at Pará, situated only 65 miles from the ocean. Manáos, rather than the coast ports, increasingly became the centre of its Brazilian activities in the years immediately before 1914. This was accentuated, when in 1912, a small engineering shop was acquired and the Amazonas Engineering Company established.

The Brazilian agencies were fortunate in having a succession of highly competent managers, under whom they developed into an important element in the company's business. They were more than offices controlling the Booth Steamship Company's interests, at their respective ports; for they inevitably developed a merchanting activity of their own, despite the company's policy of not engaging in such business where it clashed with that of local merchant houses. The Booth establishments became the most important coal distributors on the Amazon, handling in Pará alone, by the early eighteen-nineties, some 1,600-2,000 tons a month. In addition to coal, there was kerosene and softwood from America, and, in an attempt to wrest its import from the Germans, cement. In this country and in America, the various subsidiaries of Alfred Booth and Company arranged for the purchase of goods for Brazilian merchants and for the sale of some of their merchandise : sugar and rubber in New York, nuts in Liverpool and London. Although small in size compared with the shipping interest, the agencies became successful ventures once the rubber boom developed. That at Manáos made a loss of £10,000 in the early years of the 'nineties, when the business activity of the interior was still relatively undeveloped; but in 1901 when the total profit of the new company amounted to only £71,000, half was contributed by the river agencies. At the time of the amalgamation they were grouped together under the title of Booth and Company and operated as a subsidiary of the Booth Steamship Company.

The monopoly thus created by the two Liverpool lines in the Amazon trade did not, however, go unchallenged. After the defeat of the French companies in the early 'eighties, at a cost of £10,000, there appears to have been no further attempt by individual steamer concerns to enter the trade for some fifteen years. Sailing vessels continued to exert a pressure, especially in the carriage of bulky goods; but they decreased in number year by year, more markedly in English than in European or American ports. In 1857, they had represented 86 per cent of the tonnage entering and clearing in the foreign trade of Liverpool : in 1906 this proportion had fallen to 2 per cent. And as the economies of large steamers became general, so the differential in freight rates between the two types of vessels narrowed. At the end of the eighteen-nineties, the inflow of Italian immigrants into Brazil brought Italian ships into the Amazon, while ships of the American Prince Line began to call at Pará on their northward run to New York. The first intrusion appears to have been short-lived and the second was effectively countered by the use of deferred rebates.

The most determined attack came in 1902 from the Hamburg-America Line under the control of Albert Ballin. This company first appeared in the trade in 1900, when, by a friendly arrangement, the Booth's monthly sailing from Hamburg became a joint service between the two companies, the German line agreeing to proceed to the West Indies for their homeward cargo. When the agreement ended early in 1902, the Hamburg-America Line made a great effort to capture a larger share of the North Brazilian trade, and began sending ships fortnightly to London and Liverpool. There immediately ensued a strenuous 'rate war', while the introduction of German ships into English ports was countered by the sending of Booth line vessels into the German trade between the Central Brazilian ports and Hamburg. In the most lucrative branch of this, the carriage of coffee from Santos to Germany, rates were forced down from 25s. to 15s. a ton. Dr Ballin then appealed to the Central Brazilian Steamship Conference for support, but this was refused, due largely to the influence of Messrs. Lamport and Holt; and thus encouraged, the Booths settled down to a long fight. By September, however, the German line, already weakened by a similar earlier struggle with the De Freitas Company, withdrew their ships from the English ports and agreed to suggestions put forward by the Booths for the pooling of European freight and passenger earnings. The final negotiations were conducted by Charles Booth (Junior) and his brother, A. A. Booth, Charles Booth and G. M. Booth being in New York. 'It has been an exciting day,' wrote Charles Booth. 'After your two messages and my replies, as we waited hour after hour, one could not help pacing up and down at times. Then at last the short conclusive satisfactory message came and we metaphorically threw up our hats in the air and shook hands all round.' The final result of the struggle was the establishment of a pool of freight and passenger earnings from Liverpool, Antwerp and Hamburg, to be divided in the proportion of 70% to the Booth Line and 30% to the Hamburg-America Line. There was also to be an agreement on freight and passenger rates. The struggle cost the company £45,000-£50,000; but the new arrangements worked extremely well for the next decade, although not without some lurking suspicions as to German expansionist policy in commercial matters. In 1913, a still more far-reaching agreement was signed between the Booth Line and the Hamburg-South America Line and embodied in a printed document of some length: but the war intervened before eighteen months of its ten-year period had elapsed. 'An agreement of such kind,' wrote Ballin's biographer, 'was only feasible when a particularly strong feeling of mutual trust existed between the two contracting partners, and Ballin repeatedly declared that they looked upon their agreement with the Booth Line as the most satisfactory of all he had concluded.'[4]

The effect of the control thus exercised by the Booth Steamship Company over the trade to and from the Amazon River was to maintain freight rates at remarkably steady levels. Originally experimental, they had, subject to the competition of sailing ships in the carriage of bulky cargo, been determined by what the market would bear. For more valuable shipments, and for passenger transport, there were few changes. 'We worked on a tariff,' explained Charles Booth Junior to the Royal Commission on Shipping Conferences, 'for a great many years without ever altering it and that was the tariff when I came into the business (1893). There have been certain alterations both up and down, but when agreement with the Hamburg-America Line was made we went very carefully into our rates, and compared them with what other lines to the southern part of Brazil were charging, and endeavoured as far as possible to assimilate our tariff to theirs.'[5] It was argued, with a good deal of justification, that as a consequence of this control over ocean shipments to the Amazon, freight rates were 'scientific', reasonable, and because steady, favourable to the shipper: and with increasing rubber prices, this indeed must have been so. The possibility of competition made the company adopt in 1895 a practice of the Mid-Brazilian Conference in the granting of deferred rebates, and in New York of ordinary rebates. But the practice, abandoned during the Great War, while useful against the occasional intruder, was found of little value against a determined attack; especially where, as in the case of German merchant houses, a nationalist feeling entered into business.

In retrospect, the element of monopoly appears more in the exclusion of other lines from the Amazon trade than in the freedom to manipulate freight rates. Regard had always to be paid to the level of general freight charges. In the early years of the shipping company, this had been enforced by the formidable competition offered by sailing ships for certain im-

[4] B. Huldermann, *Albert Ballin*, p. 83.
[5] Charles Booth's evidence is to be found in the Report of the Royal Commission on Shipping Rings and Deferred Rebates, *British Parliamentary Papers* 1909, XLVIII.

portant categories of cargo: in the years 1900-1914, when the growth of steam tonnage began to show signs of over-expansion, it was compelled by the lurking threat of determined steamer intrusion. Hence, 'freights (rates) cannot be set without regard to general rates, even if we have no opposition to face'; and in the year of low general freight rates, 1909, it was noted, 'a monopoly (as ours practically is) can only be operated in a liberal spirit, and this applies to rates of freight as well as facilities, especially when there is around us such a mass of hungry tonnage with mouths watering at such freights as the *Crispin* has just earned'. It is noteworthy, however, that each major stage in the development of the company occurred during a fall in general freight rates, which drove foreign lines to seek new cargoes by calling at the busy Amazon ports, and by so doing compelled an expansion in the tonnage provided by the Liverpool lines. Within this relationship between freight rates to and from the Amazon and those subsisting generally, the opposition of tramp steamers was met by the obvious advantages of regular liner service. In years of low freight, the Booth Steamship Company could afford to quote below trampship rates for large shipments, provided they could be carried in small amounts.

With the rapid growth of the company's tonnage between 1895 and 1914 went a corresponding increase in its shore establishment. In 1900 the offices of the company were situated in 30, James Street, Liverpool. Here J. R. Webb (the secretary), A. E. Garland (manager) and F. G. Heise (the accountant) with a clerical staff of fourteen persons transacted the business of the firm. There were, in addition, seven outdoor staff and five engineers. At the amalgamation of the Red Cross and the Booth lines, the clerical staff of the sister concern was absorbed into the new company: when Charles Booth (Junior) succeeded his uncle as chairman in 1912, the office staff amounted to sixty-five persons, housed since 1908 in Tower Building, Liverpool. On the death of A. E. Garland in 1904, the posts of manager and secretary were combined, but were again divided in 1911, when W. L. Collins was appointed to the latter position.

At the company's main ports of call there were similar administrative developments. In London, a passenger office was opened in 1903 at 8, Adelphi Terrace, the head office of the Manáos Harbour Ltd; at Havre an agency was formed in partnership with J. M. Currie, and a marine superintendent appointed to the port; while at Oporto and Lisbon, substantial interests were held in the agency operating there under the title of Garland, Laidley and Company. The importance of Cardiff as a coaling port led, in 1904, to the establishment of a marine superintendent and coal inspector there, and, as in all marine superintendent posts, a captain—R. M. Evans—was appointed.

In the marine department—that connected with the maintenance of the fleet—the decade before 1914 witnessed the final separation from the kindly care of the Holt organization. In the early days of the shipping interest, supervision of this work had fallen to Charles Booth; and under the guidance of the Holt brothers he had performed the work from drawing up ship's specifications to ordering table wine—'which can be done very well at 8d. per bottle'. The process of setting up a separate marine department had commenced with the appointment of a superintendent engineer in 1873, but much of the work continued to be carried out by the personnel of the Ocean Steamship Company for another thirty years. In 1901, the marine superintendent at Liverpool was Captain William Isaacs; Captain William Beckett was superintendent engineer, Captain Johnson the shore captain, and L. G. Pearson the superintendent steward. Three years later, the company acquired its linen department—with its darners and fine menders—and at the same time its own medical department. All these came with the development of the fleet and especially with its passenger service. By 1912, apart from a fully staffed marine department —now with its naval architect—there was a travelling superintendent caterer, a number of ship's orchestras, a staff of twenty surgeons and an equivalent number of female nurses.

The ships of the first Booth Steamship Company sailed from the Brunswick Dock, Liverpool, but after 1901 a new series of berths were obtained on the east side of Queen's Dock, close to the site where the first ships of the original partnership had been built. The last vessel of the line to use the Brunswick Dock was the *Amazonense*, which loaded there on May 29, 1902.

The new site, however, soon proved inadequate for the volume of freight loaded and unloaded, and in December, 1906 the whole of the south side of No. 1 Branch, Queen's Dock, became the permanent berth of the company at the height of its prosperity. 'In those days, a Booth liner was frequently seen in the Mersey. They were greatly admired for their spick and span appearance and were often voted by the ferry passengers to be the neatest on the river.'

The thirty years which had elapsed between the creation of the first Booth Steamship Company and the first World War had thus seen a remarkable expansion of the business. In 1881 the value of the four ships belonging in part to Alfred Booth and Company was £67,058; in 1901 the assets of the Booth Steamship Company amounted to £501,874, in addition to £66,424 in lighters, tugs and coal stocks on the Amazon; in 1914 the value of the business was fully double what it had been a decade earlier. These were golden years, of which the last five of the nineteenth century were perhaps, the best. From 1896 to 1900 the average profits of both the Booth and Red Cross Lines had equalled £100,000 *per annum*. In the subsequent years of peace, this level of earnings was only rarely attained. 1901 and 1902 were poor, largely because of German competition; in 1903, 1904, 1908 and 1913 the fall in general freight rates was reflected in receipts through the Galveston service. But from 1905 to the autumn of 1907, when trade was disturbed by the American financial crash, and again from 1909 to the end of 1912, when the rubber boom was at its height, conditions were as good as they had ever been. In spite of these fluctuations, however, the new company earned £2,162,684 between its formation and March 31, 1914; and of this large sum only two-sevenths was divided in directors' fees and in debenture, preference and ordinary dividends. The remainder was reinvested in the business and represented a triumph of conservative financing.

CHAPTER VII

The Great War and its Aftermath

1914-1920

The outbreak of war found England engaged upon an August Bank Holiday. Later generations, accustomed to having the causes of the conflict traced and retraced, never fail to be surprised at this general unawareness of the catastrophe which ended a century of freedom from major wars. The partnership letters reflect the popular attitude of the time. The effects of the squabbles between America and Mexico are discussed, troubles in Ireland are deplored, as is the Welsh coal strike of 1912 and the possibility of a Russo-Austrian conflict. Of dangers of a more calamitous nature there is nothing. And so the first comment, written on July 31, 1914, is redolent of Edwardian England in its understatement: 'The European situation is the limit. We are all very anxious.'

It was perhaps less the inexorable movement of the political forces than the downward swing of trade activity after the boom of 1912, which occupied the minds of those in business in the year before war occurred. January, 1913, had seen much optimism; 'If Sir Edward Grey could guarantee a year of peace,' wrote the leader-writer of the '*Economist*,' 'which would relieve the excessive burden of armaments, a year of even greater prosperity than the last might confidently be predicted.' This confidence was not, however, shared by Gaspard Farrer, a partner in the great banking house of Baring Brothers, and a friend of G. M. Booth. There had been, in his opinion, too much municipal, national and commercial borrowing at increasingly high rates of interest. The boom of 1912 had resulted from the investment of this capital, much of which, as in American railways, had been unwisely expended. It was anticipated that the

Balkan States, Germany, Austria and Turkey, would require large loans, and thus still further force the rate of interest upwards. In addition, 'For some years the steady increase of gold output from South Africa has been coming to Europe, and very largely to London, which has had a tendency to increase prices for commodities and securities. Now, however, India is determined to secure gold, and in Gaspard Farrer's opinion, if a country like India, with well over 300 millions of population begins to want gold, and the people learn to like the metal and trust in it, many millions could be locked up by the population, who believe in the stocking theory, without anyone knowing it. He went so far as to say that India could take the whole output of South Africa for four or five years, say, £150,000,000 sterling, without it being possible to find much gold in one place. He thinks, therefore, that money is going to be scarce and dear, and that we may see at an early date a very considerable shrinkage in values.' Nevertheless 1913 would probably be a 'solid year' for leather, although attempts should be made to force down raw stock prices. Caution and the avoidance of expansion were, in fact, to be the key-notes to success in 1913.

As it was predicted, so it turned out to be; a good year for the leather trade. The average price of Surpass kid for 1913 was over $10 per dozen skins as compared with $9.75 for the preceding year, and sales increased by a million square feet. But it was the 'shrinkage of values' on the Amazon which, in these last eighteen months of peace, overshadowed the company's activities. The price of rubber continued to move gently downwards throughout 1913: Pará hard dry, which was 4s. 7d. a lb. in January, was 3s. 1d. a lb. in December. 'The Amazon Valley,' wrote G. M. Booth, 'is about to enter a grave commercial crisis. Some time between now and the next three years it will have to fight for its life'. The schemes already initiated by the Brazilians—the valorization scheme of 1911 and the Defesa da Borracha of 1912—proved of little value against the growing amounts of East Indian plantation rubber: and the company had taken an active interest in the investigations of C. E. Akers into the economic possibilities of the river. But it was recognized that chances of establishing rubber plantations on the model of those in East India, of growing cocoa and Robusta coffee, depended upon the formidable task of revolutionizing labour conditions in the Amazon Valley. The introduction of such changes would inevitably be slow and in the meantime 'the very possible fall in the value of rubber to 2s.' made a crisis certain.

These conditions were made worse by the struggles of the big financial interests created in Brazil by the rapid inflow of capital, particularly after the rubber boom of 1910. 1911-13 had witnessed, in London alone, the floating of new Brazilian issues to the value of nearly £50 million as compared with £34 million during the three preceding years. Of the concerns then created, the Anglo-Brazilian Bolivian Syndicate, under the leadership of Percival Farquhar, and largely financed by American, French and Belgian funds, was of immediate interest to the Booth Steamship Company. Owners of the Madeira-Mamoré Railway, the Amazon Steam Navigation Company and controllers of the port of Pará, it represented a new major competitive element to the steamship company, based as it was upon the up-river port of Manáos. The syndicate, wishing to develop Pará, argued that the use of tramp steamers to that port and a river service of large 'Dordrecht river boats' was more efficient than the ocean service to Manáos and transhipment there.

The development of a major struggle between the two companies was, however, cut short by the decline in rubber prices and by the growing tightness of money anticipated by Gaspard Farrer. The shipment of materials for capital construction financed in 1911-12 made the year 1913 a good one for the Booth Steamship Company, but the volume of freight fell heavily in the following twelve months. On concerns situated in Brazil, the effect of these conditions was felt earlier. By October, 1913, the value of public securities in Brazil had suffered a severe decline. The Manáos Harbour company failed to pay dividends, making 'a disagreeable but unavoidable point, and this is that for the first time outside members of the public are going to lose some proportion of interest or capital in one of our concerns'. The more speculative ventures of the Anglo-Brazilian Bolivian Syndicate were, however, more hardly hit, and rumours were current in 1914 that several of them were in the hands of receivers. On the general situation, of which Brazilian finance was a part, G. M. Booth noted in June, 1914, 'Practically since 1913 the great financial houses have been compelling a gradual liquidation and have been spreading the troubles of liquidation and shrinkage in such a manner as to avoid, one hopes, anything at all resembling the actual October 1907 crisis. For nine months, we have been living in a dangerous financial atmosphere, big concerns like Speyers, Societé Générale, the Banque du Pays Bas, all admittedly in low water. My news from France is that the Crédit Lyonnais alone is comfortable; scores of issuing houses have disappeared. The French people hold debentures of all sorts and kinds in South American speculations and are unable to get any information or redress with regard to them and here in London we have only today the fearful Grenfell fiasco'. The difficulties of the Syndicate led in the early part of 1914 to the opening of negotiations with Alfred Booth and Company for the control of the Amazon Steam Navigation Company, by the acquisition of which, it was hoped, the future of Manáos might be safeguarded. But the coming of war and the determination of the partners not to engage in further investments on the 'River' until the conflict ended, led to the withdrawal of the Booths from the discussions.

The impact of war upon the English interests was immediate. G. M. Booth, then in America, was asked to buy 70,000 sheepskin jerkins at 37s. each, and W. H. Tregoning, another partner, spent 'yesterday morning . . . wandering round the War Office on the question of finance, and at the end of a couple of hours I was so completely wound up with red tape that I could hardly stagger out of the door'. Arthur Fletcher organized a Prize Court Department to deal with ships of the fleet which might be detained by armed force. By September, 1914, the Government had commandeered the *Anselm, Clement, Pancras, Lanfranc, Antony, Dominic* and *Basil;* three months later, the *Manco* was also taken over, and the *Ambrose, Hilary* and *Hildebrand* were commissioned as auxiliary cruisers in the 10th Cruiser Squadron. C. W. Jones joined the colours, and by February, 1915, with him had gone thirty-eight members of the shipping office and two hundred and eighty from the dock's and ships' complements.

As the war dragged on, the loss of staff became increasingly felt by the departments of Alfred Booth and Company and its subsidiaries. Successive drafts to replenish and increase military forces depleted the numbers engaged in the business. By the middle of October, 1916, the Bermondsey office and leather warehouse was almost completely run by women under the management of Arthur Baxter. Among the narrower circle of the partners, war duties pressed with considerable force. Early in May, 1915, G. M. Booth became a full-time member of the Armaments Output Committee, under the chairmanship of Lord Kitchener, and for the remainder of the war a Deputy Director-General of the Ministry of Munitions. Alfred A. Booth, then Chairman and Managing Director of the Cunard Steamship Company, Chairman of the Liverpool Steamship Owners' Association, and of the North Atlantic Conference, played an outstandingly important part in the control of shipping. W. H. Tregoning, upon whom, with Enfield Fletcher, fell the burden of day-to-day control of the business in the absence of the other partners, was himself a member of the Liner Requisitioning Committee; while Captain C. W. Jones was brought from military duties to be secretary of the Shipping Control Committee. The years of war, too, witnessed grievous losses. The death of Alfred Booth on November 2, 1914, removed one, at their very onset, from whom mature advice might have been sought; in May, 1915, Paul Crompton, together with his wife and family, were drowned when the *Lusitania* was torpedoed on her homeward voyage from New York. With Charles Booth, the opportunity to return to a more active participation in the company's affairs was accepted with unqualified pleasure; for, as he wrote, 'the business holds me to its bosom with a charm unbelievable and absurd to most people, but which your wise sympathies can take in, I know'. It was not, however, to be for long. 'He worked with all his old ardour, and for long hours, against the advice of friends and doctors. But it was not in his nature to do anything by halves, and for some time the interest and excitement of the work had its old effect of making him seem younger and more vigorous than before.'[1] He was attacked

[1] M. C. Booth, *Charles Booth; A Memoir*, p. 31.

by paralysis in the summer of 1916, from which he never fully recovered, and died on November 23rd of the same year.

From its beginning, Charles Booth maintained that the war would last until the end of 1917; and he saw enough to have lost confidence in Asquith's direction of affairs. The failure at Kut and Gallipoli, the inability to pacify Ireland, all spelt for him inefficiency. 'Our Government's incompetence may bring us an incomplete victory or a practical defeat,' he wrote early in 1916. 'The Government is held together by a widespread fear (which to me is baseless) that no other Government would have a united people behind it. This situation might and, as I think, ought to "crack," but if, as is most likely, Asquith and his supporters carry on, we have to trust to "winning somehow." ' In his view, the best alternative to Asquith, was Lord Derby, supported by a small cabinet. In the event, Asquith's Government 'cracked' in December 1916, shortly after Charles Booth's death.

The reduction in staffs of the English branches reflected, in a way, the contraction of their primary functions. The management of the sheepskin business was transferred to New York in 1915, and in Brazil the war served only to aggravate the existing depression. Sailing somewhat north and west of the great ocean highway to the Argentinian ports, the ships of the Booth fleet remaining in service enjoyed a measure of immunity from attacks by enemy cruisers in the early stages of war. Until 1917, the company continued its truncated services between Liverpool-North Brazil-Gallveston and New York. The disappearance of German vessels enabled it to develop a trade to Santos and Pernambuco, particularly in American coal. But the flow of passengers sank to the merest trickle, and in a European trade based on the export of capital goods, it was inevitable that, while war lasted, there should be no marked improvement. The refusal of British shippers and merchants to deal with the German houses which predominated in Brazil was a further complicating factor. Most important of all, however, was the fact that 'on July 27th, when the armies were gathering, "Pará fine hard" was at 2s. 9¾d.; and rubber was one of the very few commodities whose price war did not drive up.' It was precisely the same in 1919 as it had been in 1914.'[2] As a consequence, even when the outward trade to North Brazil showed some improvement in 1916, the Booth Steamship Company could easily find tonnage to assist in lifting munitions and food from the congested port of New York. It was, indeed, only here that there was evidence of the expansion of the company's activities. Booth and Company became agents for the Holts' vessels calling at the port, and the dock staff was strengthened by the appointment of a marine superintendent and other staff. By the end of 1917, as the general position of English merchant shipping deteriorated under the pressure of German submarine attacks, the entire fleet was taken over by the Government at 'Blue Book Rates' and was returned to the company some time after the end of hostilities in November, 1918.

February, 1919, saw the Booth Steamship Company with 72,179 gross tons of shipping as compared with 123,259 tons five years earlier. With the exception of the *Christopher*, *Clement*, *Ucayali* and *Atahualpa*, which had been sold, the diminution—representing nine ships—was the result of enemy action. Of these losses, eight ships were sunk in 1917: the auxiliary cruiser *Hilary*, for example, while returning to base, the hospital ship *Lanfranc* in the Channel *en route* for England, and the *Aidan* with a loss of fifty-five lives. Other vessels lost were the *Antony*, *Crispin*, *Basil*, *Oswald*, *Boniface* and a new ship, the *Origen*, sunk on her maiden voyage in July, 1918. Of the gallantry of those who sailed these, and other, ships of the company, there is ample evidence; the fleet, although of recent origin, was manned by men worthy of the long tradition of English seamanship.

As the exigencies of war narrowed the scope of the shipping business, they increased the activities, the risks and uncertainties, of the American subsidiaries. The minor concerns —the Densten Felt and Hair Company and the Gardiner-Lucas Company in America and B. Cannon and Company in England —were immediately affected by the military demand for felt, glue and gelatine. The English company withdrew from the transatlantic market by the end of 1915 and concentrated on

---

[2] J. H. Clapham, *op. cit.*, Vol. III, p. 144.

H

the making of gelatine for home consumption and glue for aircraft propellers. In the major concern—the Surpass Leather Company—the immediate effect of war was to disorganize the export trade, particularly to Europe, to depress the price of raw stock, to render the remitting of money to England difficult as a consequence of the fall in the value of the dollar, and to create a shortage of the chemicals necessary for tanning. Hesitations with regard to the financing of skin purchases were removed by assurances from Baring Brothers of continued support: and as the countries of the world settled down to war conditions, many of the other initial difficulties became less important. The value of the dollar rose in 1915 and the remitting of money, which was rapidly becoming a factor of national importance with the increasing demand for American supplies, was easier. New sources of chemicals were found and exports of kid leather resumed their flow, though often by devious routes. Leather shipments to Russia, for example, were in 1916 sent from New York to Gothenburg and consigned to Transito Ltd., an organization set up in Stockholm to deal with Russian trade.

The position of the Surpass leather manufacturing business in America is best summed up in the following table:—

TABLE VI

Year	Sale prices per doz. skins Leather $	Total factory output in dozen skins	Total sales in dozen skins
1914	10.13	607,494	592,650
1915	9.96	548,747	679.454
1916	14.55	637,387	659,449
1917	20.43	605,813	556,298
1918	21.38	434,839	478,657
1919	31.15	558,540	590,620
1920	30.60	622,148	514,200

The pattern is clear. The effect of 'nerves' on the price of leather and the consequences of chemical shortages are evident in production figures for 1915. It was not until the end of that year that prices began to move upward, and they continued to do so throughout the following year, under the influence of war conditions and the flow of gold to the U.S.A. By December, 1916, the price of raw stock was powerfully affected by that for finished leather; Chinese skins being three times as expensive as they had been in 1914. The entry of America into the war in April, 1917, broke the high consumption of kid leather temporarily, and stocks accumulated rapidly from 30,000 dozen in January to 163,000 dozen in August; but demand reasserted itself in the last quarter of the year to reach a peak in the post-war boom, and then collapsed in 1921.

Throughout 1915, raw stock supplies were freely received in America and prices remained fairly steady. Disagreements among the partners of Cohn Brothers and Fuchs, the Calcutta raw stock agents for the Surpass factory, compelled Enfield Fletcher to visit their head offices at Zurich during the year; and, as a result, Alfred Booth and Company acquired a quarter-share in the firm, largely with a view to maintaining its existence. But as leather grew more expensive, the magnitude of raw stock purchases, the necessity of buying ahead of production, and uncertainty as to the duration both of the war and of rising prices, all contributed to a position of anxiety and danger. The need to maintain production at as high a level as possible for the purpose of earning much required dollars was an additional complication. Further, in 1917, the problem of obtaining skins became increasingly difficult. Supplies of Indian currency grew scarcer and for a time the difficulty was surmounted by the export of gold and silver from the United States. The entry of that country into the war, however, caused a shortage of shipping space, which materially affected the amount of skins exported to America. Both factors reduced the production of leather, and tended to maintain high raw stock prices. Patna skins which had cost $5 in 1914 were $20 in 1918. 'The key to my position,' wrote W. H. Tregoning, 'is that I am standing on a pinnacle and it is a jolly uncomfortable drop on all sides.'

In the meantime, with the effects of the continued decline in rubber prices postponed by war, and with a dangerously stimulated activity in the kid leather industry, the policy of the company was 'in general to look to a diversity of interests rather than to a reserve invested outside business as an insurance against catastrophe'. In pursuance of this policy, a suggested amalgamation with Dungan Hood and Company, an American kid leather firm, was rejected. But in 1917-18, a substantial interest was acquired in the Pavlova Leather Syndicate, whose works situated at Abingdon, near Oxford, produced large quantities of leather for the glove-making industry. The Lincoln leather works were then closed and the business transferred to Abingdon.

Of the old interests in English manufacturing companies, only those in Wade and Co., Nottingham, and B. Cannon and Co., Lincoln, now remained. At Nottingham, the most important development was the growth of chrome tannage, introduced into England shortly before the war. The use of kid leather for English boots and shoes led in 1914-1918 to a three-fold increase in production, but the total output in November, 1918, was still only 1,200 dozen a week, less than a day's work at the great factory in Philadelphia.

With the return of peace came almost eighteen months of boom conditions. In America, the demand for leather mounted, causing a sharp upward movement in values : the average price per dozen skins of kid leather reached $31.15 in 1919 and $30.60 in the following year, with a consequent strengthening of the world's raw stock markets. 'One gets almost nauseated by the position which is certainly growing very uncomfortable,' it was noted. Only sufficient skins were bought to keep the Philadelphia factory employed, and little stocks of any kind maintained; while the opportunity was taken of closing the Gloversville establishment for the purpose of modernising the plant.

In England, similar conditions existed. Shipments inward and outward were large and freight rates correspondingly high. Following a policy of carrying the trade formerly undertaken by German lines, the Booth Steamship Company bought the South Brazil service of the American Funch Edye Line, involving sailings to Rio, Bahia and Santos; a move which brought the company into conflict with two English lines, the Royal Mail Steam Packet and Lamport and Holt. At the same time, it joined with the Cunard and the Holts' Ocean Steamship Company to form a concern to run the Weehawken Piers at the port of New York. As the demand for ships was enormous—ten-year-old boats selling for £29 a ton and new tramps for £43—the additional space required to accommodate the traffic was supplied by chartered tonnage, rather than by building.

For all the subsidiary undertakings of Alfred Booth and Company—shipping, leather and engineering—1919 was a year of feverish prosperity. Towards the middle of 1920, however, rumblings of the approaching storm were heard almost simultaneously in America and England. In America they were regarded as indications of a temporary recession, but here there was 'much talk of a fall in material values'. The early months of the year had witnessed a continuation of the activity which characterized 1919. The Booth Steamship Company, finding itself unable to meet all the demands for cargo space, withdrew from the Galveston service, where government-owned American ships were providing a formidable competition. In the United States, leather prices continued high, and Patna skins, which had been $20 a dozen in 1918, were now $40, a rise partly due to demand and partly to the rise of the rupee in terms of sterling and dollars. By May, the weakening of the shipping and leather markets was evident: demand for cargo space and for leather fell steadily. Coal freight from South Wales, which had been carried for 50s. a ton in January, was down to 30s. in July; and was to be 22s. 6d. in December, by which date other classes of freight rates were also falling fast. The average price of finished leather, which had been 75c. a square foot in January, had declined to 36c. in July, and there was a rapid increase in stocks of finished material. Although the Surpass Company withdrew altogether from some raw stock markets in February, it was estimated at the end of May that, at prices then ruling, losses of up to 40% were being incurred on skins unshipped as late as April. From the American boot and shoe manufacturers came strong opposition to the reduction of prices, because of large stocks of goods made from expensive leathers which still existed on their shelves. But the downward trend thus initiated was impossible to stop, although the pace of the fall was nothing like that which occurred in England. The magnitude of the change cannot be illustrated better than in the facts that chartered vessels in 1919 and early 1920 earned 27s. 6d.-30s. per ton deadweight compared with 6s. in 1921: English lamb skins, which were bought for 21s. each in May 1920, were obtainable for 2s. in May of the following year: and that the average price of Surpass leather, which at the peak in March, 1920, was $44.64 per dozen skins, had fallen to $18.50 in December of that year.

With this sharp fall in prices, the immediate aftermath of war came to an end and the world entered into an uneasy heritage. To meet the new conditions, there was, however, an extended and altered company. To the older activities of Alfred Booth and Company was now added a third—engineering and construction. J. G. White and Company, bought in 1917, was concerned in the management of public utilities, the supply of engineering equipment and engineering and contracting work at home and abroad: and the Unit Construction Company, bought in 1919, was a recently-formed firm of building contractors in England.

Of the two older branches, shipping had altered least of all. The Booth Steamship Company had, it is true, a smaller fleet, but the Amazon agencies and harbour installations remained unchanged. There was too Manáos Harbour Ltd. and the Amazonas Engineering Company, to which the interest in the Weehawken Piers Company, New York, had been added. In leather, on the other hand, there had been a substantial transformation. In America, Booth and Company, the Surpass Leather Company and its allied concerns, the Gardiner-Lucas Candy and Glue Company and the Densten Felt and Hair Company, remained, but Charles Booth (Calcutta) Ltd had taken the place of Cohn Brothers and Fuchs as the agents for the purchase of Indian goatskins. There was also the subsidiary called Indian Hides Ltd., which distributed, in England and on the Continent, Indian finished and unfinished heavy leather. In Australia and New Zealand, Booth and Company retained their agencies for the purchase of kangaroo and sheepskins. But in England there were two important extensions. By its large interest in the Pavlova Leather Syndicate, Alfred Booth and Company had entered into the production of leather for the glove-making industry; while in conjunction with Wade & Co., Nottingham, the chrome tanning of kid leather for the boot and shoe industry had been commenced. Finally, as in America, it was concerned in the manufacture of glue and gelatine through its holdings in B. Cannon and Company, Lincoln.

In this way, the old policy of 'a widespread but generally inter-connected business, which provides a well-balanced structure' had been maintained.

CHAPTER VIII
The Leather Interests
1920-1939

The collapse of the post-war boom saw Alfred Booth and Company more deeply committed than ever to the making of leather and its allied products: and as a consequence, the firm's role in the next quarter of a century was that of an international manufacturer rather than of merchant.

This shift of emphasis, *inter alia*, was not without effect upon the character of the oldest branch of the business—that carried on by Booth and Company (London), Booth and Company (New York) with their outposts in Sydney and Christchurch. In 1920 the commodities handled by these offices were still much the same as they had been before the war. From Australia were exported kangaroo and rabbit skins; from New Zealand there was a flow of sheepskins to the U.S.A. via London, although already diminishing before 1914; from London were sent English grains and fleshes and to London came Surpass Leather. In the next two decades the extent of independent buying and selling within the world markets declined and this branch of the company increasingly assumed the function of raw stock agencies for the factories on either side of the Atlantic. But other factors were also making for change in the character of this branch of the business. The basis of the merchanting activity had been the supply of sheepskins to the small American leather manufacturers, and during the inter-war years the position of the independent middleman in this trade became increasingly undermined. Many of the large houses in the New Zealand meat trade, such as the Vestey's and Sims, Cooper and Company, established branches in the U.S.A.: while some of the bigger American leather concerns made their own arrangements in New Zealand. In New York itself, the markets for which the firm had originally been founded were disappearing

TABLE VII

THE PRODUCTION, RAW MATERIAL COSTS AND NET PRICES OF SURPASS LEATHER
(in dozen skins)

Year	Leather dressed	Average price of Goatskin $	Average price of Kangaroo Skins $	Average price of Black Kid $	Average price of Coloured Kid $	Average price of Kangaroo Leather $
1919	558,450			32.4	43.57	35.08
1920						
1921	389,050	8.51	—	15.02	16.18	20.65
1922	519,567	8.6	9.52	14.25	17.9	14.65
1923	477,727	10.53	15.45	15.5	13.5	21.22
1924	375,137	8.04	12.39	14.25	9.37	24.28
1925	307,116	9.10	12.67	15.36	18.62	26.79
1926	344,498	9.47	14.19	15.09	10.67	24.13
1927	341,379	9.78	10.87	15.52	11.48	24.10
1928	393,720	10.66	12.95	15.93	13.57	26.41
1929	435,070	10.29	13.05	16.29	13.57	24.05
1930	581,597	9.43	12.57	15.18	11.82	22.73
1931	658,189	8.43	8,24	13.06	9.55	19.72
1932	448,983	6.07	5.29	10.02	7.45	14.4
1933	478,010	4.53	5.17	10.65	8.68	15.92
1934	509,833	6.49	8.14	11.17	9.91	19.03
1935	551,506	6.06	8.56	11.88	9.5	19.54
1936	517,899	7.04	7.98	12.38	9.88	21.38
1937	493,596	7.93	8.01	13.15	11.35	23.1
1938	330,324	7.53	11.88	10.99	9.65	22.31
1939			9.54	11.68	10.37	20.75
1940			9.83	11.06		24.00
1941			11.20	11.5	10.68	24.91
1942	358,433	6.75	14.29	13.9	12.49	28.62
1943	327,253	6.83	15.23	14.77	12.42	30.09
1944	310,949	6.43	15.74	15.07	10.92	29.71
1945	265,555	7.58	15.15	16.40	9.81	30.18
1946	286,294	8.16	17.7	22.89	14.69	37.77
1947	329,542	13.28	24.59	25.34	24.97	43.27

There is a large range of raw stock and finished leather prices. The goat-skin prices given above are the average for the skins used in the production of black leather: coloured leather was made from cheaper material, usually about $2 cheaper than that used for black.

The leather trades were moving out of the 'Swamp': the characteristic customer of Booth and Company—the 'elderly rotund German, with an eye shade and gathered shirt-sleeves; and a leather apron to keep his trousers clean; radiating good temper and sound advice about leather; beaming happily through spectacles under his eye-shade, chewing tobacco the entire time'—was becoming fewer. By the 'thirties only a token of the old sheepskin import business remained. The most important customer then was G. H. Shephard and Sons of Bethel, and the sole survivor of the old staff, Tom Roche. Of the other members of this branch of Alfred Booth and Company, Frank Miller, the first representative of the firm in Australia, died in 1925; and C. E. Gardiner, who managed the business, first in America and later in London, in 1936. By this time, both Booth and Company (London) and Booth and Company (New York) were primarily engaged with the requirements of the manufacturing elements of the business, and the branches in Australia and New Zealand supplying kangaroo and sheepskins were now managed by W. Scott Stevenson and R. A. J. Barbour.

The principal products of the Booth factories were glazed kid leather and felt in America, glazed (or glacé) kid for shoes, glove and suede leathers, gelatine and glues in England. The Booths were no new-comers to the manufacturing of leather on either side of the Atlantic; what was novel in the post-war situation was the extent of their participation. It has been shown how this development affected the character of the business, but the consequences were in fact more far-reaching. When the war ended, Alfred Booth and Company found itself committed to a wide variety of industrial projects of one kind or another, each a promising field, but each with a pre-emptive right upon its capital. With the unforseen severity of economic conditions between 1921 and 1939, these claims matured, and the company, as a consequence, found itself committed to heavy responsibilities at a time of uncommon difficulty. In this way, the firm's ability to manoeuvre within the economic sphere tended to be limited by the restriction of its liquid resources. The leather interests, particularly in America, contributed greatly to this position, because they suffered in a full measure from the conditions of the time. The efforts of management were thus greatly preoccupied in maintaining the production of the great tannery at Philadelphia. Only in the making of English glacé leather was the story something of an exception to the general pattern of events.

The difficulties which beset the American tanners can be easily explained. The prosperity of the nineteen-twenties was patchy and precariously balanced, finally disappearing with the Wall Street crash of October, 1929. There was thus not only a smaller demand for footwear but an increased production of cheap shoes, which precluded much use of the relatively ex-pensive kid leather. American cattle hide leather thus gained at the cost of imported goatskins. Fashion also played its part. Shoes increasingly replaced boots: in the 'thirties the 'elasti-cised' shoe lessened the demand for kid linings: while the desire for leather in colours other than black operated against the main product of the Surpass Factory. In 1926, 31% of the leather used in American shoe 'uppers' was kid, about ten per cent less than before 1914; and although the proportion increased slightly until 1930, it was down to 31% again by 1934. Manufacturing costs, too, tended to be more rigid. The growing purchases by English and European tanners in the 'twenties maintained a relatively high level of goatskin prices; while the end of unre-stricted immigration and the growth of trade unionism con-tributed to the inflexibility of wages. The inter-war years were thus for the American leather industry 'a dog-eat-dog era dedicated to the survival of the fittest'.

The American tanners generally, and Surpass in particular, entered this new era with surplus capacity. The new factory at Gloversville, amply justified by earlier trends in the industry, proved to be, in the long run, an incubus rather than an ad-vantage. The company's strong financial position, the pressure of overhead costs, and the clinging hope of better times, kept both factories at work until the end of 1924, despite falling demand. By the end of that year, however, events forced a change of policy. Prices of leather were half those of the post-war boom: stocks were growing and losses increasing. As a consequence, the works at Gloversville was closed, output was curtailed at Philadelphia, and the total production of leather reduced by almost a third. With an average price of $14.25 for black leather and $9.37 for coloured (per dozen skins), 1924 proved to be the worst year of the decade. Thereafter, both prices and production climbed slowly, with a marked recovery in the fortunes of business, although it was not until 1929 that conditions improved sufficiently to permit the re-opening of the Gloversville factory.

The problems of the 'twenties led the partners to consider a variety of proposals. There was, for example, the possibility of amalgamation with other American tanners—eventually abandoned because of anticipated difficulties over the question of management. Hopes were subsequently based on a voluntary control of output by some form of combination among tanners and on the joint buying of raw stock. From the first of these expedients little was achieved. The Tanners' Council, established at New York in 1922, provided a useful channel for the discussion of common problems, but the variety of interests amongst the leather manufacturers prevented much effective combination. The second also was only partially successful. Attempts to co-ordinate the buying of skins for large sections of the industry failed, and with it the hopes of forcing a reduction of skin prices. But the world-wide organization built up by the Surpass Company in the pre-war years stood it in good stead and was, from time to time, used by a number of other companies. In this way, full advantage was taken of price movements in the older goatskin markets and new sources of supply were investigated. The inter-war years witnessed a relative decline in the use of Patna skins and a corresponding increase in those from Brazil; but the outstanding feature was the large quantities drawn from Nigeria. This source was first explored during the war years, and then developed substantially in the following years of peace. Buying through the London and Kano Company, Surpass took about a third of the local production of skins, thus 'making' the market in each year.

The most important factor, however, in maintaining the activity of the great tannery at Philadelphia was the finding of an assured market for part of its output. In 1924, Surpass prepared some skins for the enormous International Shoe Company, and two years later an agreement was reached by which it engaged to continue the practice on an enlarged scale. In 1927-1929 between 2,000,000 and 2,500,000 square feet of leather were made for this firm : in 1930 the amount was quadrupled and in the next two years quintupled—representing for a short time about half the factory's total output. In this way a valuable contribution was made towards maintaining employment at the Philadelphia works, and towards meeting the overhead charges of so large an establishment.

The crescendo of activity in America during the year 1929

sent kid prices to their highest point for the decade and output regained the levels of 1923. The Gloversville tannery was opened again for the making of shoe-linings and the company enjoyed its best post-war year. But prosperity was short lived. Commodity prices fell sharply in the wake of the Wall Street crash, and by 1931 the Gloversville works was again silent while the output at Philadelphia was reduced, although not on the scale enforced by events ten years earlier. As the world moved slowly out of the bottom of the depression there was a considerable recovery, made possible by the fact that the slight upward movement in leather prices coincided with extremely low values for raw stock. As a result, 1933-1936 witnessed a steady increase in production as well as the re-opening of the Gloversville establishment. But the sharp and unexpected fall in leather prices during the Autumn of 1937 brought an end to this uneasy period of activity : and coming at a time of considerable labour unrest, it precipitated the worst crisis in the American leather industry of the inter-war years.

Surpass 'in common with other companies in a similar line of business in America', it was written towards the end of 1939, 'has experienced unprecedented trading conditions, for not only did markets suddenly break in the Autumn of 1937 leaving every manufacturer with large inventories of leather which were eventually realized at a heavy loss; but on top of these bad market conditions, serious labour difficulties arose in this country during the year 1938 and leather manufacturers in particular were beset with endless labour disputes, which in some instances culminated in strikes. Our company had its full share of these labour troubles and our production was hampered for some time.' Many tanneries failed to survive the storm and all suffered severe losses. The Gloversville factory was closed for the third time—permanently—and eventually sold in 1942 : the Philadelphia factory was compelled to re-organize its production to a smaller output. And before there was time for the business to re-establish itself, the world was again divided by war.

These trials of the period witnessed many changes in the staff of Surpass as the older members died or retired. David Crompton, who had held the management of Booth's American interests alone after the death of his brother in 1915, was joined in the early years of the 'twenties by W. C. Burton. Together they controlled the shipping, leather and merchanting activities until their retirement in 1936. In the organization of Surpass, their most important task was the closing, in 1927, of the New York offices and the concentration of staff at Philadelphia where Harold Connett took over control of the factory. Thereafter, the accommodation at New York served as the centre for the senior American partners and for Booth and Company, the Booth-American Steamship Corporation and the Mersey and Hudson Wharfage Corporation. In 1936, Harold Connett succeeded to the presidency of the Surpass Company and Arthur Z. Gardiner to the control of the shipping interests.

The other changes can perhaps best be described by means of the history of the Surpass Lunch Club. 'When the Club first assembled on December 19, 1911, in that downstairs room, its wooden walls gleaming in newly painted whiteness—a choice of colour about which there was an oft-told tale—those present numbered only seven, plus one who was to be a normally non-attending member in the person of W. W. Hilt. Mr Hilt was the only real Philadelphian in the group, a Philadelphia gentleman of the old school. His special hobby, shared with some other Leather men of that period, was collecting oil paintings. He had been engaged as the Manager of the Philadelphia Sales and Finished Leather Sorting at the time this 'New York Department' arrived in Philadelphia in 1905, after being conducted since 1894 by Booth and Company in New York.

'The Wordsworthian "seven" (three still survive, of whom one is left in the Lunch Room) included Paul Crompton, who had replaced J. P. Mathieu as General Manager: C. H. Skinner, brought down from Gloversville in 1908 to be Factory Manager: Hollister Sturges in charge of the Raw Stock Department, and very often away on his travels overseas, and his assistant David V. Roche, who tended to remain identified with Booth and Company in New York and went home to Brooklyn every week-end.

'The remaining members were Fred Harrison, the Philadelphia Office Manager, who had come to Philadelphia in 1905, after an apprenticeship in Gloversville and New York: J. J.

Farley, until 1905 with the Shipping Department in New York and afterwards Manager of the same branch in Philadelphia, and E. J. White, who had been recently sent over as Chemist . . .

'Changes began in May 1915 with the departure (so quickly to be followed by the great tragedy) of Paul Crompton. Dave Roche, after being seen less and less in Philadelphia, died in June, 1918. The membership, now reduced to five, was brought up in the following year by the arrival from England of Percy W. J. Cannon and Jasper J. Bentley, both of whom joined the Raw Stock Department.

'Mr Hilt died in October, 1919, and his duties were now taken over by J. J. Farley, while John G. Russell came from the main office to head the Shipping Department.

'Further changes came in January, 1922, when Mr Harrison died and was succeeded by Philip J. Buchborn. In the same month D. W. Bolton . . . became chief engineer at Surpass and a regular member of the Club.

'The Club, as thus constituted with nine members, remained intact until the retirement of Mr Sturges in April, 1926, followed by that of Mr Skinner on September 24, 1927.

'This latter event signalled the end of the old regime, the arrival of the final contingent from New York, and the setting up of an expanded and reorganized Lunch Room.

'The new Lunch Room included eight who came down from New York, headed by Mr Connett, an additional five from the Philadelphia Factory and Office, as well as the seven left over from the old Club.

'Seven years later, in July, 1934, the adjoining Committee room, long disused, was brought into service to accommodate more members, the influx on this occasion being the heads of all the Factory Departments. With the help of this second room, it has been possible to absorb the migration from Gloversville when the factory was closed at the end of 1938, and steadily increasing numbers from various other directions. The most recent accretion was in January, 1948, when the Densten Hair and Felt Company came under the Surpass wing and sent over six of their staff. The present grand total is 47.'[1]

In England also the fortunes of the leather industry were far from buoyant. But kid and glove leathers suffered less than those made from cattle hides: profits were made by the manufacturers of the first of these articles even in the 'Great Depression', and the recovery after 1933 was marked. As far as glazed kid is concerned, one reason for this was the fact that the industry was relatively new to this country. In 1908 there had been only one English manufacturer of this type of leather—Wichelow of Bermondsey—and the initial expansion occurred during the war when chrome tanning was developed in this country. Thus the Booths, through their association with Wade and Co., were in the forefront of the industry here as they had been in America. A second reason for the growth of this particular branch of tanning lay in the continued use of large amounts of kid in English footwear. In this, English experience was in general different to that in America, where changes of fashion in boots and shoes usually precede those here. The fluctuations in demand for different types of leather during these years have been well described by the historian of Clark's of Street. In 1920, 'Clark's shoes were made of black glacé kid, black patent leather, box and willow calf, with a little dark nigger and bronze glacé, and no suede at all. By 1924, the picture had changed entirely. Glacé had become outmoded and the only blacks used were for old ladies' wear. There was some calf; patent leather was still going fairly strong, but suede, in all sorts of colours, was predominant. White canvas had also become very popular, both overseas and at home. By mid-1925, suedes had become unsaleable, as also had willow calf, except for children's shoes. Manufacturers took to printing kid grain patterns on willow calf to make it prove acceptable. But glacé, especially in pastel shades, boomed and held the stage for another five years. During the nineteen-thirties there was another swing over; calf and suede came back into their own, while glacé kid became once more a "back number". This situation was maintained up to the outbreak of the war.'[2]

The domestic market for English chrome-tanned light leather was gained largely at the expense of American imports, including those of the Surpass Company. This expansion, how-

[2] *Clark's of Street.*

Rt. Hon. Charles Booth 1840-1916

Alfred Booth 1834-1914

Charles Booth 1868-1938

Alfred Allen Booth 1872-1948
(Sir Alfred Booth, Bart.)

GRANDFATHER AND GRANDSON

Charles Booth 1799-1860
(Father of the Founders)

George Macaulay Booth 1877-
(Son of Rt. Hon. Charles Booth)

Enfield Emile Fletcher 1876-1942

Tom Walter Fletcher 1880-1956

Group on the roof of Imperial House, Kingsway, London, 1946

Seated left to right: Miss K. Tipper, Miss D. Featherston, Mr. G. M. Booth, Miss I. Cattermole, Miss I. Fawn
Standing left to right: T. W. Fletcher, O. S. Penton, J. S. M. Booth, D. M. Booth
Sgt. Clark, L. H. Seager, J. W. Booth, P. W. Crisp, Sir Clement Jones, Sgt. Sullivan, E. Booth

Housing Estate in Liverpool designed
by Sir Lancelot Keay

Flats in Wandsworth

'*Dominic*' alongside Iquitos Muelle, 1928
'*Aidan*' at Antonio Lemós, in the Narrows above Pará, 1924

High Water

Low Water

EARLY LEATHER PERSONALITIES

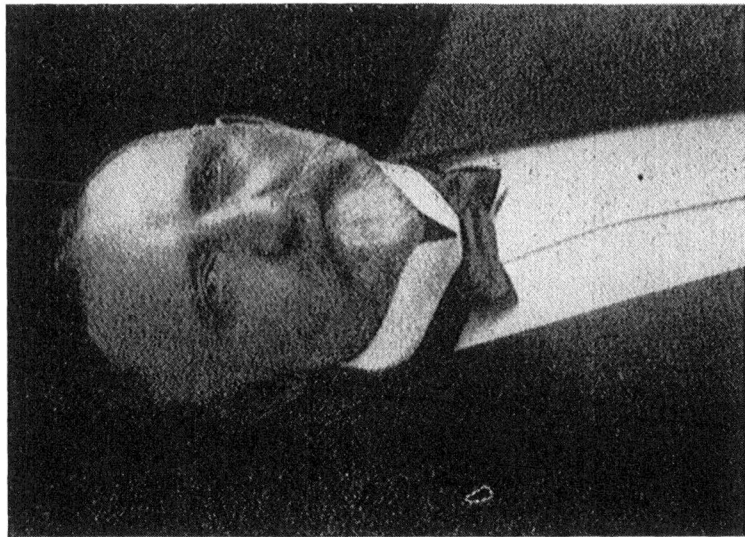

Charles Wade 1856-1924

J. P. Mathieu 1854-1918

Women Pulling Wool in the Fellmongery, Abingdon.   1914-1918 War

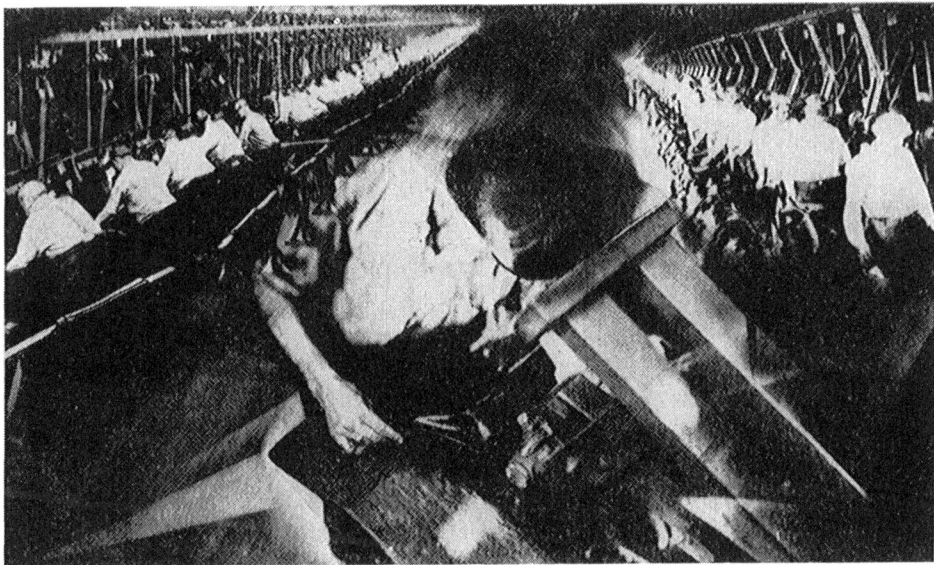

THE GLAZING ROOM, PHILADELPIA

(N.B. The rather strange lighting effects are due to this photograph
probably being a time-exposure)

THE GLAZING ROOM

We step through a door. It is shut behind us. At once our ears are assailed by a bedlam of sound . . . drumming . . . pounding . . . quivering . . . and it is some time before we become sufficiently composed to look around us.

We are surprised to find that quite in contrast with the incessant din, there is not the slightest confusion. We are in an immense room, the Glazing Room, that covers more than an acre of ground. Four long rows of heavily built, heavily braced Glazing Machines face us —noisily at work.

These machines are of two types, differing in the character of their duties—'side' and 'finishing' machines. Both types use solid glass cylinders as burnishing tools with which to hammer down the slide swiftly over a skin held on a leather strap by the worker. These cylinders, 5½ inches long and 2½ inches thick when new, are made of a heavy, frosted glass (periodically re-frosted to maintain their burnishing power) and are so worn by their constant sliding on leather that when they are discarded after three years of service they have lost a full inch in their diameter.

To the 'side machines', soft, freshly seasoned skins are brought for their first lustre. They are then sent back for a reapplication of seasoning and again put through a 'side' machine. And then, after going through a special Surpass process, the skins come to the 'finishing' machine (built to work under a slightly greater strain and to produce a richer brilliance) for the final glaze . . . and when a skin leaves the 'finisher' it has that lustrous, impeccable sheen characteristic of Surpass Glazed Kid. If it hasn't, a 'sorter' returns it for more attention.

———

ever, proved no easy task because of the established reputation of the imported leathers. 'The following,' it was written, 'is the sort of thing that happens when you try to sell a line of English kid to a buyer from an English shoe factory :—

> You spread the bundle in front of him. The buyer turns it over in silence, skin by skin, feeling the folds with his finger and thumb.
>
> Next he extracts a skin from the bundle and sets to work to spoil its flanks with his nail, latchkey, pencil or anything handy; then he opens a pocket knife and rips a piece of the leather off; smells it; and eyes it closely.
>
> At last, still bending over the bundle, he looks up at you sideways with an incredibly cunning air and says, 'Were these goods made in America or England?'
>
> You reply proudly, 'At Nottingham.'
>
> That is enough. Although a minute before he had not known its country of origin, and had in fact to be told, he now turns away from the bundle with every look and gesture of disgust known to the stage, and mutters, as though the world were a sad place, 'No, I don't want to see any more.'

Nevertheless Wade and Company were, by 1922, selling to some of the foremost of English boot and shoe manufacturers, amongst whom were Somervell of Kendal, Riley of Stafford, and Sears of Nottingham.

It was not until after 1932, however, that the English industry succeeded in finally establishing itself in a position of superiority vis-a-vis its American competitor in the United Kingdom market. This it was able to do because of two favourable conditions. During the preceding decade the high price of raw stock effectively prevented the English tanners from using the better class of raw material. In 1921, for example, the Nottingham factory tanned Amritzar and Bombay skins, later abandoned in favour of those from Nigeria. The collapse of raw stock values in the 'thirties permitted the English tanners, to their great advantage, to enter the market for the better type of skins. Secondly, the imposition of a 10% duty on imported leathers greatly helped the industry and this protection was further increased by a devalued pound. For these reasons there

I

was a sharp reduction in the quantities of American kid leather entering Great Britain with a consequent increase in the market for that produced at home.

During the 'twenties the Nottingham factory tanned about 1,000 dozen skins weekly, and increased production in the following decade by between 50 and 60 per cent. In this process of expansion, the English concern had the benefit of advice from the Surpass Company both in improving manufacturing technique and in the buying of raw stock. But the flow of technical information was by no means in one direction: the fine results obtained by Nottingham in coloured leathers, for example, enabled the English company to assist the Philadelphia factory in this particular matter. Here, as in America, however, the period was characterized by the absence of any important technical advance and increases in productivity were largely obtained through improvements in organization and management.

The stories of the two other units within the Booth organization conform to very much the same broad pattern of business conditions—a modest prosperity after a troublesome passage in the 'twenties. The first of these, the Pavlova Leather Company, although of relatively recent origin occupied a site of a long-established tannery at Abingdon. Acquired by Alfred Booth and Company in 1921 the business then consisted of leather manufacture—particularly of fine doeskin glove leather —together with a trade in sheepskins and wool. This fell-mongery activity did not last long after the post-war boom, and the buildings erected for this purpose were eventually leased to the M.G. Car Company, for the assembling of motor cars. The making of high quality glove leather continued, however, to be a major item in the company's output. The skins— mainly those of lamb and sheep—were 'finished on the flesh or "suede" side', and apart from sales to glove makers also found an outlet in the shoe and leather clothing industries. A proportion of the skins were split into a grain and a flesh; the grain 'being tanned into a skiver' and used for bookbinding, bag-linings and fancy goods of one kind or another. The markets for all these products were, in this period, found not only at home, but also in the U.S.A., Canada and the Continent of

Europe.

The second unit in this country was B. Cannon and Co. Ltd., established in 1865, at whose works on the west bank of the River Witham, at Lincoln, were produced glue, size and gelatine. Originally jointly owned with members of the Cannon family, the company became a full subsidiary of Alfred Booth and Company in the 'thirties, when the last of the founder's family retired from the business. The basic raw materials used came from two sources. The most valuable was the 'Wet Glue Stuff', consisting of waste from English tanneries: the second was the 'Dry Glue Stuff' imported from India, South America, Africa and Egypt. Until the formation of the Glue Manufacturers' Federation in 1934, conditions in this highly competitive industry were dominated by the supply of native raw material which fell far below the requirements of the producers. Its price, therefore, was high and out of proportion to those of the final products. With the emergence of the Federation the supplies of 'Wet Glue Stuffs' were divided between the various glue manufacturers in proportion to their output, with a consequent improvement in the prosperity of the industry. The allocation received by the Lincoln works under this arrangement amounted to about 4,000-4,500 tons annually. The firm had a wide variety of markets ranging from the industries processing food and manufacturing medicines, to those making abrasives, sports equipment and engaged in building and decorating.

The 'twenties thus saw a change in the role of Alfred Booth and Company in the leather trade. The status of independent merchants in skins largely disappeared and the buying organization became closely integrated into the needs of the English and American tanning companies. The decline in the New Zealand sheepskin trade was paralleled by the end of the experiment in selling Indian hides in England and the Continent through the Indian Hides Company. Although the Charles Booth (Calcutta) Company ceased operating in the early 'twenties, a former member of the staff, Mr Roland Marks, was by the late 'thirties acting on behalf of Surpass as agent for their large purchases of Indian goatskins. It was as an international manufacturing concern that Alfred Booth and Company entered the second World War. As such their largest interests were still centred in America, where, although the Gardiner-Lucas Candy and Glue Company had been sold, there still remained the important Surpass Company and its associated concern, the Densten Felt and Hair Company. On this side of the Atlantic there were the fully-owned Pavlova Company and B. Cannon and Company and the interests in the flourishing business of Wade and Company.

CHAPTER IX

The Booth Steamship Company

1919-1939

The Company's fleet in 1919 consisted of eighteen ships, representing 72,149 gross tons, or just over half the tonnage existing in 1914. Casualties had been particularly heavy among its larger vessels and, in common with other lines, the age of the surviving ships greatly increased their running costs. The sea-going staff included 24 captains, 61 navigating officers, 93 engineering officers, 20 chief stewards and 20 surgeons. Elsewhere within the company's organization there had been little change. At Liverpool there was a clerical staff of 138 persons, in addition to the workmen of all kinds employed on the maintenance of the vessels. On the Amazon itself, apart from the harbour at Manáos and the muelle at Iquitos, the loading and discharging of ships involved the use of a considerable number of tugs, lighters and pontoons. The supervision of this equipment fell to the agencies operating under the title of Booth and Company (London) Ltd., with their European staffs at Pará, Manáos, Parnahyba, Ceará, Maranham and Iquitos. There were also large interests, already described, at the port of New York; and the outside agents who attended to the welfare of the ships calling at the ports of the Continent of Europe and the United States.

The return of peace was marked by the final redemption of the £300,000 debentures which represented the balance of the purchase price for the old Red Cross Line. The Booth Steamship Company thus became, in 1921, the sole property of the Booth family and their associated preference shareholders. The members of the Singlehurst family, who had been directors since the amalgamation, retired from the Board and were replaced by E. E. Fletcher and W. H. Tregoning. Charles Booth, son of Alfred Booth, who had succeeded his uncle as chairman in 1912, continued in that office until his death in 1938. He was then succeeded by his son, John Wells Booth, who, entering the firm in 1926, had, jointly with E. B. Deyes, been its manager since 1933. During the 'twenties the post of general manager was held by F. G. Heise, with whom for a time C. K. Butler-Stoney acted as technical manager. On the former's retirement in 1929 he was succeeded by Jasper Moon, who continued until 1933. Like J. R. Webb in 1918, the successive general managers and managers were appointed to the Board on resigning their posts. Thus F. G. Heise became a director in 1929 and Jasper Moon in 1933. E. B. Deyes became a director in 1939 but remained an active manager of the company until 1946.

The accession to the unencumbered ownership of the Booth Steamship Company, however, coincided with profound changes in the conditions of trade, especially to North Brazil. The months immediately after the war saw immense activity in all South American ports as markets were re-stocked after four years of interrupted commerce. With the prices of new and second-hand ships at exorbitant levels, the company met the position by the use of chartered vessels; and also by relinquishing the homeward voyage via the Gulf of Mexico, because of lack of space for the Galveston cargo. But with the end of the boom in 1920, the trend of events in the Amazon area, foreshadowed in 1910-1913, reasserted its course. Cultivated rubber from the plantations of the Far East had greatly increased in quantity during the war; and was now not only cheaper to produce than that collected from the jungle, but was itself subject to over-production. As a result, Brazilian rubber, which had accounted for 47% of the world's supply in 1910, only occasionally exceeded 5% in the 'twenties, and never more than 2% in the 'thirties. The fall in its value was equally drastic. At the height of the pre-war rubber boom 'Best Pará Hard' had commanded 8s. 9d. a lb.: in 1920 it was down to 2s. and to 9½d. in 1921-3. The relatively prosperous years of 1925-6 witnessed something of a recovery but by 1932 the world price of this raw material had further declined to 2½d. a lb. There was subsequently a slight increase from this abnormally low level, although, except in 1937, wild rubber never again commanded more than 7½d. a lb. until the second World War. The expansion of the rubber trade which had dominated economic activity in the Amazon basin between 1894 and 1914 thus ended with the war, bringing in its train two decades of relative stagnation.

The effects of the fall of rubber prices were, however, local rather than general. The economic history of Brazil during the nineteenth century is characterized by a series of cycles of prosperity and depression based upon world demand for particular commodities. Cotton had been dominant in the early part of the century, followed by sugar and rubber. In the nineteen-twenties it was the turn of coffee; and the demand for this crop, particularly in America, meant that 'these years were marked by new and higher levels of prosperity and trade. In each of the years 1924-29 the value of exports was greater than at any time in the country's history with the exception of the peak year 1919. This healthy trade condition plus the resumption of foreign capital investments in Brazil enabled the milreis to remain fairly stable during the decade.' The total quantity of Brazil's merchandize trade, which had averaged 6,433,000 metric tons in 1911-13, reached 7,738,000 metric tons in the years 1927-29. The boom period came to an end with the Great Depression, when the volume of trade fell by almost a half. This, in turn, resulted in the depreciation of Brazilian currency, which added to the confusion in which the country's economy found itself, in common with those of most other nations. It was not until 1936 that affairs began to right themselves and the volume of trade resumed its former magnitude. The position in North Brazil was, therefore, in strong contrast to that of the south for much of this period. The region might be said to have represented the depressed area of Brazil during the inter-war period.

As such, there was not only less buoyancy but also marked changes in the post-war pattern of trade to the Amazon. There was, in the first place, a smaller volume of cargo and passenger traffic. Lower incomes meant less demand for imports and this was reinforced by the absence of much new investment in the area. The only major scheme of this kind was the vain attempt made by Henry Ford to establish a rubber plantation on the banks of the Tapajoz, a tributary of the Amazon. It is thus not surprising that the company's chairman should state in 1928 that 'since the war the trade with North Brazil in which the company is principally engaged has shrunk to less than half the pre-war figures.' And the years which followed brought little substantial improvement. The same was true of the passenger traffic. The number of richer inhabitants wishing to visit Europe was smaller; fewer also were the opportunities of employment and hence the number of immigrants. In January, 1929, the company made an agreement to carry Polish peasants from Gdynia to Bocca del Tambo, but this was an isolated instance of a once much larger flow of immigrants. The passenger figures illustrate the position well:—

TABLE VIII

	Europe to Brazil		Brazil to Europe	
	1st Class	3rd Class	1st Class	3rd Class
1910	2,412	8,234	2,494	4,880
1911	2,559	9,900	2,640	6,432
1912	2,353	7,813	2,307	5,987
1913	2,104	5,544	2,257	5,312
1914	1,389	2,545	1,797	5,985
1915	904	2,660	852	3,401
1927	369	1,869	466	1,380
1928	412	1,507	422	1,535
1929	316	1,266	409	1,394
1930	327	1,081	318	1,217
1931	263	748	228	1,361
1932	261	711	306	947
1933	231	720	246	695
1934	211	409	187	459
1935	218	499	219	599
1936	203	644	174	629
1937	219	693	207	610
1938	224	261	180	546

As a consequence of these conditions, the demand for cargo space was more seriously affected in the voyages from Europe to Brazil than in those either homewards or coastwise. There were other factors, too, which had much the same result. Coal shipments fell because of the increased use of oil: and Brazil's ability to produce a widening range of foodstuffs meant that a smaller quantity of onions and potatoes were imported from Portugal. The growth of the United States as Brazil's largest trading partner was also not without its effects. While in the 'thirties, when the company ceased calling at the North European ports, Germany's share in the commerce to this part of the world increased.

In this way, the general position was radically different from that existing earlier. Before 1914, the problem with regard to cargo space had centred on finding an adequate homeward freight: thereafter it consisted in obtaining sufficient outward shipments. This had one interesting technical consequence. The dearth of outward cargo left space for the carriage of coal for use on the homeward journey, thus delaying the change from coal to oil in the ships of the Booth fleet.

Apart from the absence of rubber, the cargoes carried from North Brazil continued largely unchanged. There were the forest products associated with the extraction of vegetable oils and waxes; the most important of which were babassu, Brazil nuts, oiticica oil and carnauba wax. Brazil nuts, as an item of consumption, had also an important market in this country, and an advertising campaign carried out after 1932 by the company and other interested firms greatly helped the sale of this commodity. Difficulties of inland transport limited the development of Amazonian timber supplies, but shipments of Peruvian mahogany began in 1930. From the coastlands of Maranham and Ceará came castor seed, maize, and other products. In the 'thirties also, there was a marked increase in shipments of cotton and cotton-seed from these provinces. Further contributions (in both directions) came, from time to time, from the agents of the Harrison Line, when no Harrison ship was available.

All in all, the carrying trade to North Brazil was perhaps more severely affected by post-war conditions than that on most other routes to South America. Still, the difficulties which characterized this route differed little from shipping generally. The world's steamship tonnage in 1931, largely because of American, Scandinavian and Japanese building, was seventy-five per cent. higher than in 1914 'with little more trade to carry than before the war'.[1] Competition was thus fiercer and freight rates correspondingly lower. Further, many of the ships which sought employment were supported by subsidies, paid

[1] R. H. Thornton, *British Shipping*, p. 197.

by governments determined to create new merchant navies to assuage national pride. All this reacted to the disadvantage of British shipping which before the war had been the world's greatest carrier. The Booth Line itself encountered this form of competition with the re-emergence of German economic activity in South America, especially in the 'thirties when German-Brazilian trade received a powerful impetus from a barter agreement concluded in 1934. In this way, the position of the North German Lloyd Line, which had been calling regularly at North Brazilian ports since 1925, was greatly strengthened. As earlier with the Hamburg Line, a friendly arrangement was made in 1936 for the division of the trade. Under this the Booths gave up their German voyages and the North German Lloyd their's to England: while ports jointly served in Western Europe were pooled. At the same time, the Booth agencies in North Brazil took over the handling of German ships and their cargoes.

The situation which faced the Booth Steamship Company during the inter-war years was, therefore, one of considerable complexity. Until 1937, the world's supply of shipping substantially exceeded the demand for its services. Against this background the company were engaged in a trade which had greatly declined in volume, but with a fleet which, because of war losses, had been roughly reduced in proportion. The ships which comprised this fleet were, however, old and expensive to operate, at a time when declining freight rates called for new and more efficient vessels. On the other hand, the growing trade of South Brazil offered opportunities of expansion which might also remedy the lack of balance between homeward and outward freights in the North Brazilian trade.

To resolve this situation by a bold policy required the investment of large sums of capital: and it was the inability to find this money, in the conditions of the time, which ultimately determined the course adopted by the steamship company. That events should have turned out in this way was largely the result of the uncertainties entertained during the war as to the future of the North Brazilian trade. These doubts had been important factors in the decision to enlarge the Booth interests in leather, engineering and contracting by the use of Alfred

Booth and Company's reserves. In doing this, the partners were acting upon the experience of the previous fifty years which had demonstrated the strength of a diversified business. There were therefore sound grounds for thinking that the anticipated difficulties of the steamship company would be eased by the revenue expected from the new branches of the business. Unfortunately the economic climate of the inter-war years proved bleaker than anything hitherto encountered. As a consequence, when it became possible for the steamship company to specify a requirement, the resources of Alfred Booth and Company were already committed because of the uneven prosperity of the leather and building trades. In these circumstances, the range of opportunities available was limited. They rendered impracticable any ideas of expansion into new trades, and enhanced the difficulties of adjustment to the new conditions within North Brazil.

In the event, this adjustment was achieved by a skilful management of time and circumstances. During the depression of 1922 to 1924 six of the older ships were sold, representing 22,965 gross tons, and were replaced between 1927 and 1930 when trade was improving. The first step was the purchase of the *Dominic* in 1927, followed by the building of three large cargo liners. Of these the *Basil,* and the *Boniface,* were constructed by Hawthorn Leslie and Company at a total cost of £218,000, and the *Benedict* by Cammell Laird at Birkenhead. The same firm was also employed in the construction of a passenger and cargo liner, the *Hilary,* of 7,000 gross tons, at the cost of £219,000. The spectacular decline of shipping activity during the Great Depression saw the sale of a further eleven ships, amounting to 47,800 tons. The replacement of these vessels began early in 1934, when Cammell Laird were again chosen to build two ships, the *Clement* and the *Crispin.* In the following year the *Anselm* of 6,000 gross tons was constructed by William Denny and Brothers; and the programme was completed by the purchase of the *St Oswald,* renamed the *Dunstan.* At the end of the rebuilding period the fleet consisted of nine vessels amounting to 46,500 gross tons, all of them new or almost new.

The policy thus pursued meant that, except in 1920 and

1931, a rough adjustment was made to the volume of freight with little laying up of ships. At the same time, by the use of these new and technically more efficient ships, operating costs were considerably reduced. This considerable administrative achievement was facilitated by the employment of chartered vessels for seasonal rushes of cargo and during the short-lived booms in trade. The regular use of charters was to some extent a reflection of the limited resources available to the steamship company; but it was also a consequence of the fact that it was often cheaper to charter than to operate Booth ships. And the continued use of such vessels was only possible because of the established position of the Booths in the North Brazilian trade. The prices at which ships could be obtained give a clear picture of the state of the shipping market during these years:

	Per ton deadweight		Per ton deadweight
1919	27s. 6d.–27s.	1927	4s. 1d.
1921	6s.	1929	3s. 9d.–3s.
1922	6s.–5s. 6d.	1930	2s. 10d.
1923	4s. 6d.–4s. 3d.	1931	3s.
1924	4s. 4d.–3s. 10d.	1932	2s. 3d.
1925	3s. 7d.	1936	2s. 10½d.
1926	3s. 9d.–6s.	1937	5s. 3d.–5s.

Charters were made use of in most years, and in some their employment was extensive. Thus in 1934 there were twelve chartered voyages, thirteen in 1935, fifteen in 1936 and nineteen in 1937.

The reduction in the volume of trade inevitably meant the abandonment of the elaborate sailing schedules of earlier days. In the nineteen-twenties and 'thirties, the usual route for the cargo vessels consisted in a voyage from England and the Continent to North Brazil, followed by one or two sailings between North Brazil and New York, and a return to England via the Continent of Europe. Booth steamers from New York sailed as far as Bahia (in contrast to the Liverpool line, which did not go south of Ceará, because of a considerable trade in cocoa and for some time in case-oil, owing to the lack of storage for oil at some of the Brazilian ports. The second line from New York arose from the rights bought from Funch Edye in 1919, which first resulted in voyages to Buenos Aires, but for most of the inter-war years the terminus was Rio Grande do Sul, southernmost port of Brazil. The passenger ships, now reduced to two in number, continued to operate the service between Liverpool and Manáos, calling *en route* at Oporto, Lisbon, Madeira and Pará; the round voyage taking some seven weeks. Among the passengers were considerable numbers on cruise to the Amazon, attracted by the phrase 'A 1,000 miles up the Amazon', coined by W. S. Cann, the passenger manager. As both passenger and cargo liners sailed from Liverpool, it became possible to carry out normal repairs and maintenance at home, which involved a considerable saving in costs as compared with prices, for example, in New York.

Equally inevitable were the consequential changes in shore establishments at Liverpool and elsewhere. In October, 1919, the company vacated its old berth in Queen's Dock for less commodious accommodation in No. 2 King's Dock, Liverpool. At each of the two stages in the replacement of tonnage, the marine superintendent's department on the dockside found itself over-manned and its personnel was reduced. The decline in coal shipments led to the closing of the Cardiff agency in 1924, and in the same year, on the death of Dr H. Bushell-Gore, the medical department was disbanded. Doctors and nurses were thereafter retained only for the passenger ships. Not all the dockside services, however, contracted. The stevedoring and porterage departments, founded in 1914, were formed into a separate company in 1924, under the style of the South-End Stevedoring and Porterage Company. It was thus in a position to act not only on behalf of its parent company but also for other shipping lines. In the six years ending March 31, 1938, the average amount of cargo handled *per annum* amounted to 135,000 tons; and the venture proved in every way successful.

The river and coastal agencies in North Brazil also maintained a substantial, if reduced, activity throughout the interwar years. At the outbreak of the second World War, they were, in geographical order from east to west: Ceará, Parnahyba, Maranham, Pará, Manáos, and Iquitos. At each port the company maintained its own offices and houses for the administrative staff. At Pará, the Booth building was a modern three-storey structure, completed in 1940, near the waterfront. As the policy of the company had been from the beginning one of self-sufficiency, there were both staff and equipment for the handling of vessels and cargo. The steamship company had its own tugs and lighters; and at Pará, Maranham, and Ceará, repair yards for their maintenance. With the development of Manáos as the major river port, the ship and machinery repair establishment had been organized as an independent unit, the Amazonas Engineering Company, which undertook work outside that provided by the needs of the Booth Line.

The great sister project—Manáos Harbour—with its investment of over a million pounds, was more severely affected by economic conditions of the inter-war years than the river and coastal agencies. During the first decade of the twentieth century, its gross earnings had been approximately £186,000 per annum; between 1921 and 1940 they were rarely as much as half this sum, and often less. The principal reason for this was, of course, the fall in tonnage using the harbour installations: but the position of the English investor was made worse in the 'thirties by the depreciation of the Brazilian currency. As a result, the income of the company, while adequate to maintain its property, left little over for the payment of interest on the capital so employed.

In the United States, on the other hand, that outpost of the Booth shipping interest, the Booth-American Shipping Corporation, enjoyed a substantial measure of prosperity during the inter-war years. As it has been shown, this independent organization grew out of the agency earlier carried on by the original office of Booth and Company in New York, partly because of the steamship company's increasing business, partly because of the work entrusted to it by the Blue Funnel Line. Side by side with the New York steamship agency, another company—the Mersey and Hudson Wharfage Corporation— owned jointly by the Booths and Alfred Holt and Company was set up in 1922 to provide dock and stevedoring services. This anticipated and eventually paralleled the South-end Stevedoring and Porterage Company which operated at Liverpool, the other terminal of the great trans-Atlantic shipping route. In addition to providing stevedoring and other dock-side services, the Mersey and Hudson Wharfage Corporation rented, at different times, piers for the berthing of vessels at Brooklyn and Staten Island, New York.

In looking back upon the years between the wars it is impossible not to be impressed by the striking contrast in conditions then as compared with those of the quarter of a century which preceded 1914. This is as true in the American leather interests as of the steamship company. The rising tide of prosperity in the earlier period had carried forward both enterprises in an impressive manner: its subsequent ebb brought forth difficulties which required great skill and enterprise to surmount. In the circumstances it was inevitable that the business of the steamship company should suffer some decline from the high levels of 1900-1914: but the position inherited with the return of peace in 1918 was maintained intact throughout the twenty years which followed. Earnings were generally much less than in the peak years of the great Amazon boom, and only in 1924-26 and in 1935 did they reach figures at all comparable to those of Edwardian days. Nevertheless, depreciation was continuously earned and a number of new ships paid for out of profits. In all, over a million pounds was invested in this way, and by the outbreak of the second World War the trade of North Brazil was served by a modern and efficient fleet. This in itself was a noteworthy achievement.

CHAPTER X

The Unit Construction Company
1919-1939

As ship-owners and as builders of harbour installations Alfred Booth and Company had long hovered on the borders of civil engineering without directly participating therein. The decision to cross this border was the most radical of the plans adopted at the end of the first World War: and from it grew the Unit Construction Company which, today, forms a major element in the Booth organization.

The first venture into this new branch of activity was taken in 1917 with the acquisition of J. G. White and Company. Founded in 1899 as the English branch of a well-known American engineering and finance house, J. G. White and Company Inc., the business was managed by a group of American engineers led by W. C. Burton—later a partner of the Booths—and by A. N. Connett, father of Harold Connett, later President of the Surpass Leather Company. During the early years of the century the firm had carried out important constructional work on tramways, light and power plants both in England and abroad. Of these, large sections of the L.C.C. tramway system, those at Bournemouth and Belfast, the Amsterdam light railways, the Adelaide and Calcutta trams, and the Lacroze tramway system in Buenos Aires, were typical examples. At the same time a subsidiary concern, the Waring-White Building Company, erected many well-known London buildings, such as the Waldorf Hotel, Selfridge's Stores, the Stoll Theatre, and the Royal Automobile Club in Pall Mall.

The two companies first came into contact with one another in connection with J. G. White and Company's work at Pará and Manáos. The Booth Line carried the constructional material, and later the coal, for both the Pará and Manáos power stations and the light and tramway systems; and by

1910 G. M. Booth was already a member of the board which controlled these installations. When, therefore, an opportunity of acquiring the English company presented itself in 1917, Alfred Booth and Company were well acquainted with the general character of the business, and bought it as part of the policy of broadening their interests at home, and particularly in South America.

'When the first World War came to an end, J. G. White and Company had developed in various ways, with many subsidiary companies. Among these, Whites were responsible for a large organization called the "International Light and Power Company" with tramways and power companies at Caracas, Merida, Parna, Curityba and, of course, the Pará and Manáos properties. In addition, there was formed an export and import merchant business with South America, known as "J. G. White Commercial Company Ltd.", with eight or more branches in South America.'[1]

But here again events belied hopes. The decline in South American prosperity, and the marked fluctuations in English industrial and commercial activity, resulted in considerable disappointments. This involved a reduction in the merchanting and engineering sides of the business, and, as a consequence, J. G. White and Company became increasingly a finance company engaged in the management of earlier investments. The firm's interests were further reduced in 1928-9, when the upward swing of financial activity in America enabled much of the South American holdings to be disposed of with advantage. What was left of the business was then re-sold to its founder— J. G. White. Two years later it was again acquired by G. M. Booth, not, this time, as part of Alfred Booth and Company, but as a private venture. In this Mr Booth was associated with Mr A. Drummond and Mr W. B. Burton-Baldry, and later with Mr Ian Fairbairn. The company was re-named White, Drummond and Company Ltd., and remained, as it does today, in its old offices at 9, Cloak Lane, E.C.4.

During the nineteen-thirties, the engineering side of the new company continued to diminish. By the beginning of the second World War it was small indeed: consisting mainly in the ad-

[1] *Booth Bulletin.*

K

ministration of the Manáos Tramway Company, and other tramway and lighting installations in the East, especially in Singapore and Shanghai. This decline in the original work of the company was balanced by the growth of important interests in the field of unit trust investment, through a subsidiary concern, the Municipal and General Securities Company Ltd. Here, a very successful and important enterprise was gradually built up, which today manages four trusts, having a total capital of approximately fifteen millions sterling.

The second—and as far as Alfred Booth and Company are concerned the major—step into the sphere of civil engineering was taken with the acquisition of the Unit Construction Company. Here again the firm was not in origin a Booth concern, having been founded early in 1919 by the Crittall Manufacturing Company, makers of metal windows and furniture. The original intention was to build houses for the company's employees and to overcome the shortage of bricks by using concrete blocks of standard sizes in dwellings of unit dimensions. It was from this feature that the company derived its name. The head office was at 246, High Holborn, W.C.2, with N. V. Foulis and A. D. Harris—both fresh from war service—as its managers. When in September, 1919, the Crittall Manufacturing Company decided to sell its subsidiary, the majority holding in its shares was acquired by Alfred Booth and Company. The head office was moved to 168, Regent Street and the capital increased in successive steps until in April, 1920, it stood at £50,000. By the end of that year, at the beginning of the post-war building boom, the new addition to the Booth organization had achieved a business turnover of £35,000 a month, and had begun to undertake substantial contracts for local authorities in various parts of the country.

Under its new ownership, the Unit Construction Company set out from the first to be a large-scale contracting firm. As such it was an integrated concern providing from within its own resources many of the major skills required in this type of work. During the early years of its existence, the making of cement was carried on by a subsidiary, the North Essex Portland Cement Company, and the quarrying of gravel through the Rom River Company. These were sold in 1925, and although new gravel pits were opened at Romford, Dagenham and else-where, cement was henceforth obtained from outside the company. At first the whole of the administration of the company was centred in London, but in 1923 a branch office was opened at Liverpool which allowed of a devolution of responsibility for the northern contracts. The management centred in London upon A. Dale Harris, D. Adams and T. G. Randolph, together with Harold Tregoning (until his death in 1930) and G. M. Booth (as Chairman) from Alfred Booth and Company. Also responsible for developments in various parts of the country were J. Ellis and H. Picken, the latter of whom built up a re-markably efficient house-building organization in Liverpool over many years. Control on the individual sites lay in the hands of an agent, who, with power to use a local banking account, and with the assistance of a staff of peripatetic clerks, was responsible for the work on hand. Much of the skilled and unskilled labour was recruited locally—often upon the insist-ence of the local authorities for whom the building was being done; but, as the work of the company became increasingly based on two centres, many of these men became virtually per-manent employees of the company. The specialized crafts—plastering, glazing, painting, plumbing, tiling and slating—also remained outside the organization and were obtained by a system of sub-contracts, again usually placed locally.

Throughout the early nineteen-twenties, the company en-gaged in public works contracting as well as in house con-struction. Industrial buildings were erected for a variety of firms; stations were built for the Metropolitan Railway at Farringdon Street and Wembley Park; and the Walton Institute for the West Derby Board of Guardians. Of more importance were the large number of sewerage and water schemes under-taken for local authorities in various parts of the country. A major sewer tunnel in London and thirty-five miles of water mains for the Newport Corporation, Monmouthshire, were the largest individual contracts, but similar work done at Lither-land, Stainforth, Doncaster, Wednesbury, Darleston and Broad-stairs was also of considerable magnitude. In house building the first major contract was that for the Southport Borough Council in 1920-23, which amounted to £221,000. This was

followed in 1922-24 by work valued at £613,000 for the Liverpool City authorities and the building of 340 houses for the
Edinburgh Corporation. The Liverpool contract was noteworthy for two reasons. It was the first of a long series undertaken for this authority and it enabled the company to experiment in the building of 'no-fines' houses. These are constructed
by 'pouring a concrete mixture containing no fine aggregate
between shuttering made up of moveable steel panels and allow-
ing the mixture to harden'. In this way new sources of labour
and material were brought into use to supplement the
traditional house building materials. Other areas in which
houses were built in these years included Risca and Newport
in Monmouthshire, Rugby, Gloucester, Roehampton, Dudley,
Walsall and Welwyn.

By 1925, the Unit Construction Company had completed
contracts to the value of approximately two million pounds, a
substantial achievement for a newly-established firm. In its
public works undertakings, however, the company met with
less success than in housebuilding, largely because of serious
unforseen hazards encountered in some of the contracts. In the
laying of water mains at Newport, for example, large boulders
continually broke the excavating machinery, and trenches had,
accordingly, to be dug by hand. At Prestatyn, where sewers
were being constructed, high tides and running sands also
created serious difficulties. As a consequence the company
withdrew from this field and concentrated upon large-scale
house building.

In this specialized form of construction work, it benefited
greatly from the expansion of investment after 1926 by both
local government authorities and private individuals. After a
considerable fall in 1924 and 1925, the number of new houses
within the first of these categories rose sharply in 1927 and
1928; and although there was a subsequent decline, the level of
output remained well above the low figures of 1924-5. But the
fall of investment by public authorities was more than made
up by the remarkable boom in private building after 1928. As
a result, the building industry enjoyed a high degree of activity
for much of the inter-war years, contrasting vividly with conditions in the older basic industries of the country. In the decade

1919-1929, 1,500,000 new houses were erected in England and Wales; while the 'thirties saw this figure increased by approximately eighty per cent. With its branches in London and Liverpool, the Unit Construction Company was well placed to take advantage of this spate of activity. The metropolitan area attracted much new light industry during these years; and both cities embarked upon substantial slum clearance programmes. Because of these circumstances, the company was able to concentrate its efforts in two well defined areas; only in Brighton in 1933, and later at Cambridge, was building undertaken outside London and Liverpool. In all, the Unit Construction Company completed contracts to the value of approximately ten million pounds between 1925 and 1939.

Of the two regions, Liverpool was the more important. Here, work to the value of six million pounds was undertaken during the interwar years, as compared with three and three-quarter million pounds in the London area. Some of the contracts performed for the Liverpool Corporation were very large indeed. At Walton, Strawberry Lane and Norris Green, 3,000 houses were erected in the late 'twenties: 1,700 at Dovecote in the early 'thirties: 2,326 at Woolfall Heath and a 1,000 at Speke in the last years of the decade, and the early years of the second World War. In London, the greatest period of activity occurred in the 'thirties, and, in contrast to Liverpool, the building of flats formed a large proportion of the buildings put up. Of the major schemes of this type, those at Kennington, Dorset Road and Newburn Street, Lambeth, and at Tulse Hill, Brixton, are particularly noteworthy. In the building of houses, the Unit Construction Company undertook a large number of smaller contracts for urban district councils on the outskirts of the Metropolitan Area until 1936, when it obtained its first large undertaking—1,400 dwellings at Hanwell and Kenmore—for the London County Council. In 1938 it commenced work on 2,800 houses at Chingford and in 1939 on 1,500 at Kidbrooke, both for the same authority.

Although by far the largest part of the Unit Construction Company's business lay with the local government authorities, it was inevitably drawn into the boom for privately owned houses. This again took place within the London and north-western regions, thus reinforcing the organizations established there. The first venture of this kind was at Hayes and at Uxbridge in 1929. On the first of these sites, 88 houses were erected and on the second 48. All were, within a short time, sold and occupied. The purchase of these properties was facilitated by a procedure which later became common in the industry, and which was adopted on later development schemes of the company. 'The great obstacle in the way of many families who would have liked to buy their own houses through building societies had been, for many years, the initial payment of a lump sum equivalent to between a quarter and a third of the value of the house. Various attempts had been made to get over this difficulty, but it was not until the 'thirties that an arrangement by which this payment was reduced to 5 per cent. of the value of the house came into frequent use. The basis of the system was extremely simple. The building societies advanced as usual up to 75 per cent. of the value of the house against the personal security of the purchaser and the security of the house itself. In addition they made a further advance which might bring the total up to 95 per cent. by arrangement with the builder against sums deposited with them by the latter. The purchaser repaid the whole amount with interest in the usual way, and in the process the builder's collateral was redeemed. By 1938 this system or some variant was so widespread that possibly half the business of some large societies was transacted on this basis.'[2]

The depression which followed 1929 postponed further schemes of this character until the building boom of the 'thirties was well under way. During these years the experience of the two schemes at Hayes and Uxbridge was also not entirely satisfactory. The depression caused some people to give up their houses and as many as 30 out of the total of 88 at Hayes were sold and re-purchased with the assistance of the Abbey Road Building Society. The revival of private development began in 1933-4 with two small schemes. Forty-four houses were built at Liverpool and in the following year eight larger houses were erected at Cobham, Surrey, financed by the Leeds Building Society. The same year saw the beginning of the two major

[2] Marion Bowley, *Housing and the State*, p. 175.

schemes at Liverpool, which, with the public authority contracts, were to occupy the company until the outbreak of the
second World War. By agreement with the late Lord Salisbury,
an arrangement was made for the development of 59 acres of
land at Broadgreen, Childwall, near Liverpool. By November,
1935, 705 houses and 18 shops, with the necessary roads and
sewers had been constructed; and most of the dwellings
occupied. The second scheme was set on foot in September,
1936, when 64 acres were purchased at Speke, near Liverpool,
at a cost of £500 an acre. By the outbreak of war, 127 large
houses, 60 medium and 472 small houses, together with 20
shops, had been sold.

'Assure him,' wrote Charles Booth in 1887, 'that we can be
very patient in working for success.' This patience in the second
and third generations of the Booth family was reflected in the
establishment of a new branch of business by the outbreak of
the second World War. By this date, the Unit Construction
Company had become one of the major components of the
British building industry, with contracts, both completed and
in hand, amounting to many millions of pounds. In England
this branch of the business had become the largest direct employer of labour in the Booth organization. And, as earlier
generations of the family had learned the business of merchanting in the counting-houses of Liverpool, so members of the third
generation, in the persons of Edmund Booth and Albert Fletcher,
were learning the techniques of the Company's new venture in
Liverpool and London.

CHAPTER XI

The Second World War
1939-1945

If the first great conflict of the century sprang into public notice with startling rapidity, the same cannot be said of the second. As early as January, 1936, thoughts on the possibility of hostilities were creeping into partnership letters. 'What are the odds on a general European War within two years?' enquired W. C. Burton from New York, 'I think if it comes it will settle in the negative the hopes (that) any of us anywhere may have of a reasonable world for the next hundred years.' And the months which followed deepened the pessimism both in business and in politics. A disturbed Europe, a disorganized Far East, 'South America practically one vast moratorium', the slow industrial recovery in the U.S.A. aggravated by the uncertainties of the New Deal legislation and by mounting labour unrest —all contributed to making business in these years an uncertain and unremunerative activity.

The declaration of war in September, 1939, involved a new factor in the possibility of air attack. With this in mind, part of the London office was transferred to Abingdon, from whence C. F. Little continued to transact the business of Booth and Company with Australia and New Zealand, and P. W. Crisp part of the work of Manáos Harbour Ltd.: while the obvious difficulties of maintaining the peace-time system of co-ordinating committees at Adelphi Terrace led inevitably to a delegation of management. G. M. Booth in London, with Enfield and Tom Fletcher in Liverpool, continued to deal with the financial aspects of the company; Sir Alfred Booth undertook special war indemnity work. Matters arising from the factories at Abingdon and Nottingham were divided between Clement Jones and D. M. Booth: O. S. Penton became responsible for some of the central affairs of the company while continuing his connection with B. Cannon and Company, Lincoln, and the Russells of Hitchin; while the departure of Lt.-Commander J. W. Booth to join the skeleton Ministry of Shipping left the management of the Booth Steamship Company in the hands of E. B. Deyes. In this way, the central control of the firm was maintained throughout the war, although irregularity of contact with the outside world threw greatly increased responsibility upon those in charge of the subsidiary establishments in America, Brazil, India, Australia and New Zealand. 'Correspondence,' wrote G. M. Booth in 1940, 'becomes more and more as it was sixty years ago. I remember my cousin Tom Fletcher, the father of Enfield and Tom of my generation, telling me that on receipt of a mail from America he always read two mails backwards.'

As in 1914, there was a steady drain of staff to the forces. Many had joined the territorial units, among them J. S. M. Booth, who, during the 'thirties had been learning the leather business on both sides of the Atlantic. The Booth Steamship Company, although no longer a major unit in Liverpool shipping, again made its direct contribution to the Navy. The *Crispin* and the *Hilary* were detailed for naval duties in which the latter played an especially distinguished role in the successive campaigns of the war. Fitted out as an Ocean Boarding Vessel in January, 1941, she served in home waters until April, 1942. Early in 1943 she was again commissioned for naval service and was engaged in the invasion of Sicily, acting as a headquarters ship wearing the flag of Rear-Admiral Sir Philip Vian. In September, 1943, the *Hilary* took part in the Salerno landing, as the flagship of Commodore G. N. Oliver; a year later as the flagship of Force J, she was present at the Normandy landings, where she again wore the flag of Rear Admiral Sir Philip Vian. The other ships and their crews continued their gallant work as part of England's merchant fleet. As in the Great War, losses were grievous. The *Clement* was sunk by the *Graf Spee* off Pernambuco in October, 1939; the *Crispin*, the *Dunstan* and the *Empire Endurance* were lost in quick succession in the early months of 1941, and the *Fort la Maune* in February, 1945.

Further, at the request of the Government, the 685th Artisan Works Company, Royal Engineers, was largely formed from men of the Unit Construction Company early in the war. Consisting of six officers, a warrant officer, forty-two non-commissioned officers, and two hundred and forty men, it was commanded by Major Edmund Booth, and numbered among its ranks others whose parents had long been associated with Alfred Booth and Company—Albert Fletcher, Edward Tregoning and Dale Harris. On the evacuation from France in 1940, twenty-four members of the works company were posted missing, of whom all but three were notified as prisoners of war. These, including Major Booth, remained in German hands until the allied victory in 1945.

In America, the years of uneasy neutrality, which characterized the initial stages of the war, saw a great deal of pro-British activity by the staff of the subsidiary companies. Miss Margaret Siemer established a centre for the British War Relief Society in the offices of Booth and Company, New York: Harold Connett and H. H. Hegeler took leading roles in the Fight For Freedom Society—an organization of businessmen designed to counteract isolationist sentiment: while engineers from the Booth-American Shipping Corporation were seconded to the British mission engaged in buying American ships. When the war engulfed the U.S.A. after the disaster of Pearl Harbour, the widening range of economic controls made further demands upon the staff on both sides of the Atlantic. Clement Jones became chairman of the Technical Personnel Committee in London, a member of the Radio Board and of other committees dealing with technical and further education, for which work he was knighted in 1946. Arthur Z. Gardiner, manager of Booth and Company Inc. and of the various American shipping subsidiaries, became shipping adviser to the U.S. Board of Economic Warfare; and Harold Connett, President of the Surpass Company, was appointed head of the Shoe and Leather Section of the U.S. War Production Board. Both appointments were made early in 1942, and their work in the Booth companies was taken over by Michael Eland and H. H. Hegeler respectively.

In an age in which the aeroplane had made possible both air attacks and the peripatetic administrator, those who remained in business or left for government service suffered in a measure from the risks of war. The Liverpool office of the firm received considerable damage from air-attacks, and the buildings in Adelphi Terrace, which had housed Alfred Booth and Company for nearly half a century, were made uninhabitable in 1941. As a consequence, temporary accommodation for the remainder of the period was found at Imperial House, Kingsway, at Reigate and at Millbank. The movement to and fro across the Atlantic, whether on private or public business, was itself a hazardous business. 'On the whole the journey was extremely comfortable,' reported J. W. Booth of one such crossing in 1942, 'but we had one hour in the middle of the Atlantic during which I was more scared than I have ever been in any blitz. We were flying at sea level in a gale, with the machine tossing about like a feather, and at times the salt spray was actually splashing over the machine.'

The impact of war upon the business varied. It stimulated the greatest activity in shipping and building, both vital elements in the war-time economy. On leather production, on the other hand, difficulties in securing raw materials resulted in a gradual contraction of output in England and America: although, as the war continued, a shortage of leather developed and there was a considerable widening of profit margins.

Unlike the first World War, English merchant ships came under government control immediately hostilities began, and the company's responsibilities were reduced to acting as a government agent. The direct trade between England and Brazil ceased, but the existence of American neutrality did, however, allow some part of the carrying trade between Brazil and New York to be continued for some time by the use of chartered vessels. The rates per ton dead-weight for these ships rose rapidly from $4.29 (inclusive of war risk insurance) in November, 1940, to $12 in May, 1941. The entry of America into the war in December, 1941, brought this activity to an end; and thereafter the company was limited to managing its own fleet and such ships as were allocated to it by the Ministry of War Transport. These included the *Empire Endurance*, *Empire Flame*, *Fort la Maune*, *Fort Nipigon*, *Sam Yale*, and the *Empire Voice*; the last of which the company purchased in March, 1943. Voyage details and the freight to be carried were determined by the appropriate government departments and committees. These conditions were naturally reflected in the business of the subsidiaries at the great trans-Atlantic terminal, New York. Although the Booth Line had ceased by 1941 to be clients of the Booth-American Shipping Corporation and of the Mersey and Hudson Wharfage Corporation, and the ships of the Lamport and Holt Line only rarely made an appearance in the port, increasing work was obtained from the vessels which crowded into New York to carry American supplies to Europe. These included ships of theAnchor Line, of the Funch Edye Company, occasionally those of the Cunard Company, and of the Norwegian and Dutch missions. The large and increasing work done on behalf of the Elder Dempster Line led, in 1944, to the sale of part of the Booth's interest in the Mersey and Hudson Wharfage Corporation to that company.

In the Unit Construction Company, the building of houses largely ceased, and construction was directed to public works of national importance. In Liverpool and London there was much to be done in the building of civil defence shelters and later in air raid demolition work. A large number of contracts were undertaken for military establishments—at Lincoln, Watchfield and Staverton for the Royal Air Force, for example, and at Yeovilton for the Royal Navy. In this way, the organization was kept fully occupied throughout the war period. The only new development of these years occurred in 1943, when the entire share capital of Messrs. Burlow (Builders) Ltd. was acquired.

The dominant feature in the remaining branch of Alfred Booth and Company's business—the manufacture of leather and of glue and gelatine—was the supply of raw materials. And in this, the establishments in America were ultimately as strongly affected as those in England. In both countries, too, the course of business showed marked similarities. 1940 did little to alter the deep-seated malaise affecting the American kid leather industry and in England market conditions worsened with the impact of war; then, as military needs made increasing demands upon leather supplies, prices were forced slowly upwards. With the declaration of hostilities in the U.S.A. came a plethora of government controls similar to those already in existence here. Total supplies of raw stock were allocated between the two countries, but shortage of ships saw a steady fall in the amount of skins reaching English and American ports. As a consequence, it became increasingly difficult to operate the factories economically, particularly in America where the position was exacerbated by the steady pressure for higher wages. The output of Surpass fell from 19.85 million square feet of leather in 1941 to 11.71 million in 1945. War demand, however, did enable the factory to diversify its markets, particularly in the production of leather for air crew clothing. The further decline in the business of Booth and Company Inc. as the result of war conditions led to the closing of its offices at New York and their transference to Philadelphia. Miss Margaret Siemer, who had been Secretary and Treasurer of the company after the departure of Mr Gardiner, retired in 1944, on completing the move, after nineteen years' service with the Booth's American interests. Finally, the factory at Gloversville was sold in 1942.

This reorganization in America was accompanied by other developments at home. In conjunction with the other four shipping lines operating to South America—the Blue Star, the Pacific Steam Navigation Company, the Royal Mail Steam (Packet) Company and Lamport and Holts—the Booth Steamship Company entered into an agreement to establish an air service for the carriage of passengers and freight. This document, signed in February, 1944, founded the British Latin American Air Lines Ltd., of which J. W. Booth was elected chairman. Two years later, when this organization developed into the government-owned British South American Airways Ltd., Mr Booth was again appointed chairman and relinquished his equivalent appointment with the shipping company. At the same time Sir Clement Jones became a director of the British Overseas Airways Corporation.

Such considerations of post-war developments led inevitably to thoughts upon the future of the Booth Steamship Company. The experience of the years between 1919 and 1939 had shown that operating a fleet of liners in a trade to a restricted region was a precarious business. It was only with difficulty that the revenue earned covered outgoings, of which by far the most important was the capital cost of ships, and the necessary provision for depreciation. This problem became acute in the last stages of the war, when the prospect of peace brought to the forefront the replacement of war losses. There was every reason to fear a rise in building costs, which would absorb not only monies obtained for compensation and the supplementary grants under the Government Tonnage Replacement Scheme but also additional sums from the capital of Alfred Booth and Company. For this reason, and having regard to the other requirements of the business generally, it was agreed to sell the entire shipping concern, with its subsidiaries in England, America and Brazil. This was accomplished in April, 1946, when the Vesteys acquired the Booth Steamship Company, its interests in the Booth-American Shipping Corporation, the Mersey and Hudson Wharfage Corporation, the South-End Stevedoring Company and the Amazonas Engineering Company, as well as the Booth agencies on the Amazon.

Of the old interests on the Amazon, there remained only the connection with Manáos Harbour Ltd. Thus ended eighty years of ship-owning and nearly a hundred and seventy years of business activity in the port of Liverpool. There were still the widespread and important activities in skins and leather as well as a lustily growing business in the building industry. But the sale of the Booth Line partially severed one sentimental link with Liverpool in that the head office of Alfred Booth and Company was moved to London, although the largest branch of the Unit Construction Company continued to represent the family in the birth-place of the Booth enterprises.

CHAPTER XII

Booth Men and Labour Relations

_____

It is perhaps a truism to say that, what are called labour re-lations, will depend very largely upon, first, the traditions of that section of business in which the individual firm is estab-lished, and secondly upon the attitudes of its founders. The last, in turn, is an amalgam of tradition and environment, of per-sonal qualities and intellectual capacities. This is particularly valid in family concerns, where there is the direct influence of ownership as well as a strong element of tradition. In the case of Alfred Booth and Company, where there are still some who remember its founders, the work of Alfred and Charles Booth in this sphere remains the basic influence.

Both men were the products of the middle decades of the nineteenth century, with views derived from a nonconformist, radical and mercantile background. They received their train-ing in a merchant house at a time when this form of organiza-tion retained many of its older features. For, at the middle of the century, most offices of this kind still comprised small groups of clerks and apprentices, all of whom worked in close contact with their principals and many of whom were drawn from the same social strata. Nor was this peculiar to Liverpool and the provinces. Much the same characteristics applied to the commercial houses of the capital. The entire business of the London Assurance in 1831, was transacted 'by the extraordin-ary attendant (a director), the secretary, the accountant, and about a dozen clerks';[1] and there is Lamb's familiar account of the 'most munificent firm in the world—the house of Boldero, Merryweather, Bosanquet and Lacy'. Everywhere the hours of work were long but the pace leisurely. There existed a personal and intimate relationship between employer and employee.

[1] Bernard Drew, _The London Assurance_, p. 118.

Above all, 'merchanting is a big, broad, strong business, re-
quiring close attention, nerve and sound decision, carrying
large profits or large losses'; the element of personal responsibility was great.

Most of these characteristics were, very naturally, trans-
mitted to Alfred Booth and Company, and they explain in
some measure the views of its most active founding-partner.
To neither Alfred nor Charles Booth was the mere accumulation of money a paramount end: profit was a measure of
efficiency, a means rather than an end. With the younger
brother this concern with the efficiency of production was the
dominant aim of industrial policy, involving, if necessary, the
exercise of monopoly. It could be best accomplished when
capital and labour worked as a team under the leadership of a
restless, questing enterprise, which he described as 'fore-
thought, guidance, the capacity to plan, the nerve to execute,
the whole genius of mind and character, all this living source
of human welfare and progress.' This view demanded from
labour the acceptance of agreed remuneration, loyalty and a
'sympathetic interest and pride in their special employ.' The
growth of organized labour was regarded with a sympathy
born of his own radical views, a respect for its leaders, and a
first-hand knowledge of the economic conditions of its members. But where trade union activity diverged from the pro-
motion of efficient production—as in his opinion it had by
1900—he was critical of its policy. But 'the productive values
to be found in the workman's efficiency, great as they are,
cannot compare with those which may be achieved by the
bold use of capital or follow the application of genius to enterprise.'[2]

Basically as true today as when written, these views of
Charles Booth were in a large measure evolved from his experience. They represented an idealism, rational and optimistic,
for which the economic expansion of the nineteenth century
offered much support. They rested, however, upon two important assumptions. They required, in the first place, a highly
cultivated social conscience, a willingness to share the gains of
enterprise, and a sober, responsible use of economic power.

[2] M. C. Booth, *Charles Booth; A Memoir*, p. 94.

Secondly, these views implied a freedom for the deployment of capital and labour which was only tolerable, in the case of the last, as long as the economic system absorbed fairly quickly the labour made redundant by economic changes. The events of the 1920's and 1930's, as will be shown, modified the views of Charles Booth's successors in this respect. But it is interesting to note that the extension of political power, very largely accomplished through the efforts of nineteenth century radicals, of whom Charles Booth was one, provided the vehicle for the curtailing of freedom of enterprise in the interests of the economic security of the mass of workers. The consequences of his political and economic thought thus in the long run proved incompatible.

The most obvious characteristic of the old merchant organization which was carried on into the firm of Alfred Booth and Company, was the idea of an ordered training in business matters. During the 'seventies and 'eighties the company received a number of indentured apprentices at a premium of £100, of whom Thomas Christie of Fochaber, for many years manager of the New York shipping department, was among the first. The practice, however, was given up when the nature of the business developed in such a way as to provide too narrow an experience of commercial matters. But the idea of training for young men was retained in the Booth Steamship Company until 1914. Here, there existed a scheme covering five years, on the successful completion of which, candidates were given a certificate of proficiency as clerks. After 1918 much of this basic training was taken over by specialist institutions and, as a consequence, the same necessity for it, within the firm, disappeared.

More important was the maintenance of the old characteristics of close personal relationships between the partners and their permanent staff. This was based, in the first place, upon a belief that high wages and salaries, with permanency of tenure, in return for loyalty and efficiency, was in the long run the only satisfactory method of employment. 'It is to our interest,' wrote Charles Booth in 1879, on the occasion of the Liverpool dock strike, 'to get picked men, so far as we can, both at sea and on shore, and picked men are well worth the

L

extra wages.' This was amplified in the following year. 'We go on the plan of high pay and have stuck to it through bad times and good and shall continue to do so.' And in those days the choice of men reached even to the lower deck; a feature which disappeared with the growth of the fleet. Miss Emily Booth, for example, frequently visited the dock and investigated and helped any case of hardship. 'High pay' involved also liberality with regard to other conditions of work. The extent of the holidays granted to the English staff, for example, on the Amazon, was, before 1914, the subject of much criticism from other merchants there, but was defended on the grounds that the 'men were not only in better health and spirits when at work in the Amazon, but are more closely in touch with us and able to take and understand a broader point of view.'

The familiar discrepancy between English and American prices and wages, however, soon presented problems in pursuance of this policy. Thomas Fletcher, the resident partner, found New York expensive in 1880. 'Everything has gone up in value this year and New York is more extravagant than ever,' he wrote, when taking a house in 216 East 18th Street. In 1882, he recurred to the subject. 'The problem of living as compared with salaries is getting a very difficult question. Living expenses have increased awfully in the last two years.' The influence of English standards tended to keep American salaries from rising as fast as they did in other New York houses, although such was the reputation of Booth and Company that there appears to have been little change-over of staff. Generally, however, salaries and wages in America became, for comparable positions, considerably higher than in England. On the other hand, the pace of work seems to have been greater there than at home. When Alfred A. Booth (later Sir Alfred Booth) visited the U.S.A. in 1898, he reported, 'I consider that the men generally who give their work to Booth and Company are too much driven—certainly more than in England. I should much like to see things arranged so as to be easier and so that each one should have at any rate three weeks' holiday.' Such arrangements were made, but both differences persisted over the succeeding fifty years.

Secondly, 'picked men' involved careful choice at all levels.

As the American side of the business developed and came more and more under the control of American based management, the annual reports on permanent employees, including the women 'type-writers', increased in volume. The twentieth century was marked by the growing number of men entering the business, both on its administrative and technical sides, from the universities. But choosing men (and women) is a task fraught with much risk, and some mistakes were inevitable. 'The frauds,' wrote Mr Miller from Australia in 1896, 'were conducted in a most skilful and astute manner, and reflected great credit on the gentleman's university training. He was actually a graduate of Oxford.' Nevertheless, the success of the policy has been borne out by the number of the staff who, entering the firm at an early age, have become directors of its various concerns. Among them, for example, can be named, Sir Clement Jones, C.B., Paul and David Crompton, F. G. Heise, J. R. Webb, Charles Good, Benjamin Crimp, J. Moon and E. B. Deyes. It had a further important consequence. In a large and expanding family concern, especially one which persists from one generation to the next, no problem is more acute than the problem of management. Nothing has contributed more to the success of Alfred Booth and Company than its ability to attract not only young men of ability, but persons of more mature age, like W. H. Tregoning, Henry Dakyns, O. S. Penton, A. J. Robertson, C. K. Butler-Stoney, C. E. Gardiner, W. C. Burton and Harold Connett.

The creation of successive generations of 'Booth men' has not been, however, solely a result of careful selection, personal interest and high pay. The character of its founders, particularly that of Charles Booth, encouraged the expression of reasoned opinion, which is essential to the assumption of responsibility and the fostering of co-operation and loyalty. In a sense, the successful running of a world-wide business with its dependence upon the judgment of individuals in widely dispersed centres, made such a development a necessity. But the tendency was encouraged and sustained by the constant movement of staff between the various countries connected with business. As the company grew, the flow of correspondence and visits was supplemented by a system of committees—ranging from committees of foremen in Philadelphia, in the first decade of this century, to discuss technical problems of production, or of ships' captains and stewards, to central committees of directors in which various aspects of the business were coordinated.

The practical expression of this concept of a team, 'a set of men working towards one end', was the decision taken by Alfred and Charles Booth in 1871, to divide a proportion of the profits among their permanent staff in the form of a bonus over and above their salaries. In January of that year £70 was given to each senior clerk in Liverpool and New York, and £35 to each junior one. 'It is understood that what the clerks get will remain with us at 10% which I am willing to pay on all their savings and it is not to be drawn out except on some expenditure of capital, such as furniture, life assurance, or some other investment.' In the 'eighties the rate of interest on such deposits was reduced to 5% in England and 6% in America. It was a practical recognition of work and loyalty: and an incentive to thrift, the sums so accumulated being regarded as supplements to the pensions granted by the company. Until 1914, conditions were such that bonuses were paid in bad as well as good years, for Charles Booth held that the successful negotiation of depressions required as much, if not more, work than when times were prosperous.

The success of the scheme was more pronounced in England than America. This, to some extent, perhaps, was the result of different patterns of expenditure, of greater opportunities for profitable investment outside the company, and of the constant upward pressure of prices across the Atlantic. The influence of this last factor can be traced in England in the decade before the Great War. Before 1912, captains of the Booth Fleet received a relatively low fixed salary and a relatively high bonus, which by this date they had come to regard as a regular part of their salaries for current purposes. In that year, to meet the changed use of the bonus, salaries were raised and the rate of the bonus reduced.

The sums thus distributed were always substantial and in prosperous years large. During the year 1919-20, for example, £40,970 was given to the permanent staff of the steamship company and almost a quarter of a million dollars to the employees of the Surpass Leather Company. In the years preceding the world war, the scheme was extended to include engineers and stewards on the ships and all grades of clerical staffs in the shore establishments. After 1921 the long series of unprofitable years made the payment of bonuses an intermittent practice. But in 1926, the amounts accumulated by the staff of the various branches of Alfred Booth and Company amounted to between £250,000 and £260,000, some deposits having developed into large permanent investments. A maximum limit of £2,000 was then placed on all future deposit accounts, and at the request of the company the larger depositors reduced their sums by a total of £60,000. On sums up to the stipulated maximum the company continued to pay 5%. As a special security for the £200,000 remaining in the concern, a quarter was invested outside the company, and a rule made that any encroachment on this fund was to be made good before the payment of any dividend. In the 'twenties also, new pension schemes were established in conjunction with English and American insurance companies and pension rights were extended to all workmen at the Gloversville and Philadelphia factories.

As the firm grew and became increasingly employers of skilled and unskilled workmen, the application of these principles to all categories of staff became more difficult. What had been possible in the choice of seamen when only 5,000 tons of shipping were owned was impracticable when there were 124,000. And apart from the consequences of magnitude, there were peculiar difficulties. Seamen, as distinct from officers, engineers and chief stewards, contracted for single voyages, and were thus constantly on the move from one company to another. In America, much of the labour force before 1914 consisted of a 'flowing stream of Poles, Italians, Slavs and Roumanians'. Here too the element of casual labour was paramount. Finally, until the 1920's, Alfred Booth and Company were predominantly employers of American rather than English industrial labour, which in itself involved a degree of conformity to different methods and outlook in the sphere of labour relations.

The first contact with organized labour was an indirect one. In 1879, when conflict broke out between the Liverpool ship-owners and their dockers and seamen, Alfred Booth and Company joined the masters' association at the request of Alfred Holt, but with the reservation that their own seamen's wages should remain unchanged because they were specially 'picked men'. In discussions which then took place between the two brothers, it was agreed that short hours of work, wages determined by the purchasing power of money, with regularity of employment, and overtime for 'pushes of work', was the ideal system. 1879 was a year of widespread unemployment, and to Charles Booth's ordered mind the lack of an apparatus to deal with redundant labour was a matter of regret. 'The remainder must starve or go . . . this alternative is the only one we know of adjusting our labour problem in these cases which is a pity.'

It is interesting to compare this reserved acceptance of the nineteenth century economic mechanism with the change which had taken place by 1932. Faced with great unemployment in America, G. M. Booth wrote to W. C. Burton in New York, 'I have come to the conclusion that one measure, and one measure alone, is needed to start movement in the right direction and in the right way and on the right scale, and that is the immediate administration of what in England is called the 'dole'; through the endless admirable organizations which for two years have been administering private funds, by implementing these funds from the Federal treasury under certain broad regulations . . . The economic objections to the 'dole' are many, but I believe the pro's vastly outweigh the con's, and no other form of inflation does so little harm, or does rapidly so much good. For two years, the need for charity has been recognized and its administration organized on a vast scale; and there is no material difference between money so found and National money, except reasons which are all to the good.'

'For your private ear, I had an hour with Governor Norman (of the Bank of England) the day before yesterday and he blew up my scheme sky high, and said that the 'dole' had been and still was England's ruin and that the English working man was being taught not to work. I had to tell him he knew nothing about his subject. And that we with wide experience of labour on ships, on docks, in all branches of building, in factories at Lincoln, Nottingham and Abingdon, in gravel pits in Essex, in ship-repairing at Liverpool, as well as ship-building at Birkenhead, could testify that the English working man had improved out of all knowledge in the last two years.'

The first direct clash with organized labour occurred in America in 1886, soon after the small Gloversville factory had been purchased from the widow of John Kent. The 'Most Noble Order of the Knights of Labour' were then at the height of their power in the north-eastern states, and were actively campaigning for higher wages and a nine-hour working day. The rejection of these demands by the Shoeleather Association was followed by a strike and a move to establish a co-operative factory, with $25 shares for each participating workman. Julius Kuttner, as the New York manager, was most closely concerned with negotiations, but Charles Booth exercised a strong moderating influence from London. Many of the views which he later expressed in writing were already formed in his mind. On the inevitability of conflict between masters and men, unless wisdom and patience were employed on both sides, he was certain. With regard to the length of the working day, he shared the views of his contemporaries. 'On the question of nine *versus* ten hours, I am rather on the side of nine as the best working day in the present state of civilization.' A day of eight hours is, I think, too short and ten hours too long.' But, 'I don't think the nine-hour day is possible yet but it is more in accord with modern ideas of life and will come eventually.' The eight-hour day was only applicable when 'machinery goes night and day with three shifts of men'. If 'we began work at 7.30 in winter and worked until 6 o'clock, with an hour for dinner, and began at 7 in the summer and worked until 5.30, and ultimately made the day 7.30 to 5.30, I think the time question would be settled for a generation.' The success or failure of the co-operative factory was, in his opinion, the fairest test of whether the strike was well based or not; and unlike the American owners was willing to see the experiment tried. 'But first let us do our utmost to come to an agreement and to do so give the men, whether knights or not, the full benefit of every point which is just now in their favour. I think they ask for too much, but I think something more might be conceded.' It is certain that these views had little influence upon the actual situation in Gloversville and Philadelphia, but they well illustrate the attitude of Charles Booth towards some of the conditions of industrial labour. The ultimate failure of the strike and the return to work was the result of the weakness of the Knights of Labour, rather than of any conciliatory policy adopted by the Shoeleather Association.

In England, the company was not called upon to face any major disturbance amongst its workpeople. The development of unions among the lower-deck seamen was generally accepted and both sides worked with a great deal of amity. In 1911, for example, after a conference with representatives of the Sea-men, Firemen and Stewards Union, the Booth Steamship Company agreed to increase the wages of such men by 10s. a month, involving an additional wage bill of £8,000 a year. The founding of the Surpass Leather Company in 1905, however, brought the firm into close contact with the labour unrest which characterized Philadelphia during the last years of peace. Throughout 1911 and 1912, there was a series of strikes involving an attempt to impose a very uncharacteristic 'maximum or limit system with provision for turning in the surplus earnings to an association—for the benefit of a slower neighbour'. On the conclusion of one such stoppage in 1912, the introduction of a bonus system was discussed, and the then Sir William Lever's *Address on Co-partnership* was sent to the American management with the observation that although Lever had made a great fortune, his workpeople were more contented and better housed than most others. The large proportion of immigrant and highly mobile East Europeans in the Surpass factories, however, made the institution of such reforms almost impossible. But steps were taken to introduce a workmen's compensation scheme based on that existing in England under the Acts of 1897 and 1906: a surgery with a qualified nurse was established in the Philadelphia works, and a dining-room for foremen, clerical and managerial staff. This was followed by a cafeteria in the early years of the 1920's.

The traditions thus established by Alfred and Charles Booth

have been maintained by succeeding generations in economic conditions which differed materially from those of pre-1914. Thus in the commercial agencies at home and abroad, in the offices of the Booth Steamship Company and its permanent sea-going staff, in the establishments of the Surpass Leather Company, the Unit Construction Company, were groups of men and women known to the partners and forming a well-knit group of 'Booth men'. The formation of the National Maritime Board in 1919 ensured, in common with the British shipping industry generally, the existence of amicable relations between owners and men, and a notable absence of strikes. But to these generations of Booths fell the unhappy task of successive reductions in the staff of the Booth Steamship Company. This was accomplished by two economy committees, in 1923 and 1931, which carefully examined the case of each member of the firm. Those nearing retirement age were placed on pension to facilitate the retention of younger men: and almost all who were dismissed left with a sum proportionate to the length of their service.

In America, the decline in the volume of immigration and the growth of a geographically more stable labour force after 1918, enabled the introduction of pension schemes for all categories of workmen and the development of a considerable element of goodwill between management and workers. The strengthening of the position of organized labour under the New Deal in the 1930's caused much less concern to the English partners than it did to the executive directors of the Surpass Company. Indeed, the emphasis laid by Sir Alfred Booth and G. M. Booth upon the need to increase purchasing power as the surest method of overcoming the long depression made them more sympathetic to Roosevelt's experiments than their American colleagues. To the latter the industrial policy of the New Deal achieved only the raising of prices, costs and wages at the expense of efficiency and production. On the narrower question of trade unionism the respective viewpoints—reminiscent of the exchanges of 1886—are well summarized in a series of letters between Sir Alfred Booth and D. H. Crompton.

March 21, 1934. New York . . . However, the labour and union situation is getting very serious. The idea is practically to outlaw the company union and to force employees into the hands of the American Federation of Labour.

April 4, 1934. London . . . Since you wrote the dangers of a Strike in the Motor Industry has been removed, for the present at any rate, by what purports to be a compromise, though it seems to be a victory for the American Federation of Labour. I think it is inevitable that labour conditions will approximate more and more to the position which has come about gradually in this country during the last fifty years, although the development here was very greatly accelerated during and immediately after the war. Roosevelt seems to be trying to bring about overnight what has taken us fifty years. Owing to the size of the country and the much greater diversity of industrial conditions, it was natural that Trade Union development in America should have lagged behind the movement here. We are quite used now to nation-wide Unions, which work in co-operation with or antagonism to National Confederations of Employers and I do not think now that we should wish to return to the older system of smaller local unions and independent action by employers, even if it were possible.

The big Trade Unions are all bound together to a certain extent by their membership of the Trade Union Council, but that Council has no power to dictate to the various Unions, and I do not think that anything of this sort is likely to come about because there is too much independence of spirit in the leaders who manage the various industrial Unions. The Trade Union Council is rather an advisory and a consultative body. On the other side, the Federation of British Industries and the Confederations of Employers' organizations fulfil rather similar functions. I incline to think that a similar development will now take place in America and there is no fear of a country-wide monopoly Union with some dictator at the head of it; on the other hand, I think it is somewhat inevitable that Trade Unionism will attain in America an enormously increased political influence, as has been the case here. What worries us most in the American situation is a fear that a further reduction of working hours may increase your costs again and that general purchasing power will not increase rapidly enough to enable the consumers to pay correspondingly higher prices.

April 14, 1934. New York . . . I agree that if conditions as to the character of the labour leaders and also some of the employers were different, the best method would be something approaching the English method of nation-wide Unions and National Confederations of Employers. We have here, however, a great variety of races in both employers and employees, which makes combinations extremely hard to work effectively. Also you are not cursed by the great variety of Unions in the same trade that we have here, and the competition among Unions for membership, or the absolutely racketeering Union who bring gangsters from the large cities into a small locality and terrorize workers with the expectation of getting lump-sum payments from employers to call off the strike. Apart from the Washington situation and use of their influence to push the A.F.L., I would say that today the natural trend is towards the Company Union in the larger, better-run plants, and I am inclined to think that with the difficulties as to co-operation obtaining here, this may for a time at any rate be the best solution for business such as ours.

In this way, the experience of the Old World came to the assistance of the New. Even so, the Surpass Company did not escape its quota of labour troubles during the nineteen-thirties, despite the fact that the American directors claimed that their workmen were, in general, paid somewhat higher wages than in other tanning establishments. As a consequence, labour problems figured prominently in the correspondence from America during these years, particularly after the year 1934. The Surpass Factory was closed by strikes in 1938 and there was much complaint about working to rule in the later months of the following year, and again in 1940. The last agreement made before the war with the International Fur and Leather Workers' Union of the U.S.A. and Canada came into force on August 1, 1939. In it, the company agreed to a five-day working week of 40 hours: to pay overtime at the rate of $1\frac{1}{2}$ times the regular wage scale: to recognize a 'departmental seniority subject to competency' in the case of redundancy: and to allow the appointment of a shop steward. Further, future employees were required to become members of the union and the company promised to 'lay off' unionists who were three weeks in arrears with their union dues.

CHAPTER XIII

Alfred Booth and Company

The capital with which Alfred Booth and Company was founded originated in the legacies, amounting to some £14,000, left by Charles Booth in 1860 to his children, Anna, Alfred, Charles, Emily, and Thomas Booth. In this sense the firm was a continuance of two generations of merchant activity. It was thus a family business and it has largely remained so during the ninety years of its existence. In all essentials the history of the business is that of a private estate. The features of the estate have been examined and it now remains to draw these various aspects into a composite picture, by relating them to their common activity—the investment of capital; and to trace its consequences upon the functions of the parent company.

The estate has had two outstanding characteristics. In the first place it has been employed in a wide and inter-connected series of enterprises. In this respect the company has carried into the present day, something of the old tradition of the eighteenth and nineteenth century business houses. By so doing, a balance has been maintained between the proportion of capital in fixed, and in circulating or easily realisable, assets; the one representing a slow, and the other a quick, turnover of business. In this way, the estate has retained an important element of flexibility, and a consequent opportunity for manoeuvre. Equally important has been the fact that this spread of activity has tended to mitigate the impact of adverse business conditions. In the nineteenth century, leather and shipping were, at critical times, mutually supporting ventures. Steamship earnings were, between 1868 and 1878, an essential factor in the finance of the American sheepskin business, with its relatively quick turnover of capital. In the present century, the dolorous inter-war years affected glove leather far less than they did shoe leather; and, because of public expenditure, contracting and building far less than either. And this feature has been strengthened by the existence of units of business in different continents—in South America, in Europe and North America.

TABLE IX

The Capital of Alfred Booth and Company
under the partnership

Year	Amount	Year	Amount
1865	14,000	1897	297,178
1880	73,415	1898	299,555
1881	93,977	1899	327,454
1882	113,437	1900	472,407
1883	130,244	1901	492,897
1884	129,696	1902	525,497
1885	130,591	1904	552,046
1886	145,729	1905	541,605
1890	174,236	1906	564,722
1891	208,669	1907	580,945
1892	252,451	1908	582,156
1893	280,290	1909	569,633
1895	296,997	1910	574,744
1896	300,193	1911	546,032

Secondly, the estate has grown up and been maintained by the re-investment of profits. In this respect also it is typical of eighteenth and nineteenth century enterprise, by far the major part of which developed as the result of a conservative financial policy. The slow expansion of the estate in its first twenty years coincides with the establishment of the business; the rapid growth between 1879 and 1883 and again between 1889 and 1906 with the existence of prosperity in leather and shipping: and finally, a maturity, reached during the years of the Great War. Examples can be taken from either branch of the business. The valuation of the assets of the first Booth Steamship Company trebled the value of its shares in 1901; and twenty-seven years later £750,000 of undivided surpluses in the second company were similarly capitalized. In the Surpass Leather Company, on the other hand, the holdings of Mathieu and Company were liquidated from the accumulation of profits in this American concern. In a large measure, the growth of the estate in this way, was a response to the opportunities offered in the period 1890-1920. Expanding business called forth its own capital.

But the thrift, which this growth reflects, was also an expression of the world of ideas into which Alfred and Charles Booth were born, with its emphasis upon individual effort and personal responsibility. It can be seen, for example, in the manner in which members of the staff were encouraged to save by the payment of bonuses and of high rates of interest on their deposits in the firm: or the scepticism with which limited liability companies were greeted in the leather trade: 'They don't look limited in the least,' wrote Charles Booth in 1871 of one such firm, 'and seem quiet and respectable.'

But there were periods when the rate of growth was too fast for the resources of the estate, particularly in its shipping interest, where large additions of fixed capital were required at critical moments. On occasions such as these, when the first ships were built for example, or when the fleet was doubled in 1881, recourse was made to friends, relatives, and to intimate business acquaintances. In each case, relatively large sums were obtained, although the bulk of the money remained that of Alfred Booth and Company: in each case, subsequent expansion came ultimately from the re-investment of profits. The first public subscription was the partially successful debenture issue of 1901: followed two years later by that for Manáos Harbour. Here, the issues were well received by the 'solid investors of the north of England'. Thus, in the main activities of the family, other than in Manáos Harbour, subscribed capital played relatively little part in the finances of Alfred Booth and Company: and when the bulk of the preference shareholders in the Booth Steamship Company were bought out in 1928—many of them descendants of those who subscribed to the first company in 1881—the last major element of outside capital in the immediate interests of the firm disappeared. For the same reason, there has been little of the division between ownership and management, so characteristic of modern enterprise.

Of more general importance in the period 1863-1903, than the occasional call upon outside capital, were the private credit resources made available to Alfred Booth and Company. These fell into two categories. There were the short-term credits, important in the first twenty years of its existence, which were obtained from merchants in the Liverpool business community.

These loans, used to tide over temporary shortages of cash, were provided by the Holts, the Rathbones and Lamport and Holt, generally without any security. They represented assistance to young men whose ability and integrity were recognized and trusted. Risks were assumed which the banks—especially the strictly run Heywood's Bank—were generally unwilling to accept. In times of easy money the rate of interest charged was the Bank Rate : in times of stringency it was $\frac{1}{2}$ to 1% above the rate. On the part of the recipients of this trust, the responsibility of the loans was a matter of some seriousness. 'I would a great deal rather cheat the government out of all the income tax than overstep our position in an undertaking of this sort,' was its exaggerated, youthful expression.

By the 1880's, the necessity for such accommodation seems to have disappeared. This was partly the result of the growth of the second category of credit facilities—the friendly deposit of uncertain duration. This reflected the abundance of capital available in the last decades of the century and the low return obtainable on home investments. The practice, as with that of granting short-term credits, was an old one, and can be traced among manufacturers and merchants in the eighteenth century and earlier. The lending of money to the railway companies in the second half of the nineteenth century was another expression of this activity; and, in a different form, it survived in the Lancashire cotton industry until the 1930's. In common with other Liverpool houses, as Alfred Booth and Company prospered, an 'Open Account' was established, and into this account were paid such deposits. By 1880, these amounted to £44,000, at a time when the capital of the partnership was £72,000 : and it was with the aid of these sums that the working capital of the firm was largely furnished in these years. The constant flow of this finance, the fact that it was often left indefinitely, and the opportunity of borrowing elsewhere if large sums were suddenly withdrawn, made its employment in the structure of the business a safe procedure. In 1896, it was estimated that, of the £548,000 of capital and credit used in the various branches of the business, 53% represented Booth capital—the estate proper—23% that of depositors, and 5% that of bank credit. But payments into the 'Open Account' were not limited to private individuals. When Alfred Booth and Company temporarily possessed more money than could be made use of, it was generally paid into the Holt's 'Open Account'. There is unfortunately no record of the interest rates paid upon such investments; but they must have been related to those obtainable on government securities and also to the position of the company when the money was offered. There is every reason to believe that, as a method of finance, deposits were cheaper than bank credit, with its additional operating charges. The extent of these private credits seems to have been reduced in the years immediately before the war of 1914-18. For this a number of factors was responsible. The more formal structure of the company's finance enabled some recourse to debenture issues to be made: a far greater use was made of bank facilities: and with the closer adjustment of supply to demand on the capital market there was less free capital seeking a safe and remunerative employment. But loans from the Holts remained an important factor until the outbreak of the Great War.

The working of these methods of finance is well demonstrated by events in the decade 1895-1905, when the simultaneous expansion of leather and shipping placed the company under considerable strain. The existence of depression in America from Autumn, 1893, to early in 1897, caused stocks of skins to accumulate in Boston and New York; while the demand for chrome tanned kid leather involved an expansion which outstripped the resources of the American business. Consequently capital flowed to Booth and Company, New York, through resources placed at its disposal by the parent company, which, in turn, obtained them from the earnings of the steamers. The position was comfortably met in 1894, but the decision to add 15,600 tons of shipping to the fleet in 1895-6, altered matters considerably. It was fortunate that, in these years, there existed in England, genuine, if patchy, conditions of prosperity. In 1895, there had been great activity in gold-mining investment, and in the following year, 'everybody seems to be making money out of something and consequently are good humoured about losses'. The Rochdale flannel trade had rarely been so busy, glue-making was profitable, and many were fast becoming rich out of the bicycle boom. Credit was thus plentiful and cheap, and bank assistance was obtained to pay for two ships built in 1895; while some further relief was gained by redrawing consignees' bills of exchange and by discounting notes of American customers in New York. But at the same time, pressure was exerted on Booth and Company in New York to increase their remittances, which drew from Julius Kuttner a mild protest against 'dispensing as much as possible with modern banking facilities which are made use of nowadays by even the very rich houses.' Yet, with these expedients, the profits of the steamers saw the company through 1896: 'It is not too much to say that both this year and last we should have had to ask for further assistance under pressure of necessity, if it had not been for the large earnings of the steamers.'

As the early months of 1897 slipped by, conditions improved in America, causing some movement of stocks, and a consequent easing of the financial position. At home, the continued prosperity of the Amazon trade, allowed, with the help of small loans from the Bank of Liverpool, the transfer of four small ships of the Booth Steamship Company to the Empreza Line, and the establishment of the Iquitos Steamship Company. During the next two years, the finance necessary for additional tonnage, other than that obtained from the reinvestment of profits, came from deposits. At the end of 1897, £11,000 was lent by one of the Holts' smaller companies, and in the following spring £60,000 was received from their Ocean Steamship Company. In 1899, a further £20,000 was deposited by shareholders in the Booth Steamship Company at 4½%. By this time, conditions had so improved in America that a return flow of capital was set in motion, enabling Alfred Booth and Company to lend the Booth Steamship Company £60,000 for the purchase of new vessels. All such loans were of short duration, repayable, and in fact repaid, from anticipated profits.

This temporary easing of the strain was facilitated by two other factors. Increasing use was made in America of banking credits, provided first by Kidder, Peabody and Company and later by Baring Brothers, for the purchase of goatskins; and secondly, by the issues of debentures on the amalgamation of

M

the two shipping lines. But German opposition with its consequent losses in 1902, a bad year in leather in 1903, together
with the demands made by Manáos Harbour again resulted in
a tightening of finances. By the middle of the year, the position
was such that Charles Booth was induced to set aside work on
his social investigations and devote almost his entire attention
to the business. For this purpose he took rooms at 40, Sydenham Avenue, off Ullett Road, Liverpool, in September, 1903.
The immediate difficulties were met by a loan of £50,000 from
the Bank of Liverpool, with a possible extension to £75,000
if required. This proved to be the last special loan of the period,
for, with the turn of the year, conditions improved and the
company moved into calmer financial waters. The period of
rapid expansion was over: the output of Surpass leather had
been doubled, the new steamship company was firmly established, and the harbours at Manáos and Iquitos opened. In June,
1904, Charles Booth went up to Oxford and there 'The Prime
Minister's letter (with its offer of membership of the Privy
Council) actually reached me . . . on the eve of my D.C.L.
degree, and I really am overwhelmed. I am afraid my little stock
of dignity will quite run out but I must hold up as well as I can.
In truth it is a very great honour, shared as regards men in my
kind of position by very few. The congratulations I receive add
immensely to it.'

Back in business, the remainder of the year was taken up by
the preliminary negotiations for the unifying of the Gloversville and Philadelphia factories into a single company and the
eventual buying out of J. P. Mathieu and Company. In December, he wrote to New York, 'We discussed the matter fully and
have decided that we can entertain no further expenditure on
commitments on tonnage until the *Anselm* is paid for. That is
that we will make no further move until next year. On this
subject I feel very strongly. We must get out of the very
strained position in which we have been so long and become
independent of anticipation of profit and special bank credits.'
It had been a full ten years in all respects. But, throughout, the
financial policy had been consistent: the private character of
the estate had been maintained and, as far as possible, its development had been from its own resources.

Hitherto, circumstances had limited the recourse to bank credits. The position changed with the growth of Surpass. The purchase of nearly seven million skins annually, representing upward of five million dollars in value, involved too great a burden for the resources of the business. As a consequence, the dependence upon bank credits became a regular feature of the leather business from the first decade of the century onwards. The needs of the factory at Philadelphia were supplied from American sources, but skin purchases were financed by four-monthly credits provided from this side of the Atlantic. In the inter-war years, the employment of 'modern banking facilities which are made use of nowadays by even the very rich houses' was extended to all other branches. It was, and is, particularly important in the activities of the Unit Construction Company, where a large rapid turnover leads to equally large variations in the use of bank credits.

As time passed, the growth of the estate and the increasing variety of its features, both at home and abroad, necessarily involved changes in the way in which it was organized. And as always where there is a division of labour, it is possible to trace the gradual concentration of the parent firm upon the central function of the business—namely the initiation and control of financial policy. In this respect, the history of Alfred Booth and Company is in many ways a microcosm, in which most of the stages through which the English banking system emerged during the eighteenth century from its merchant origins are reflected.

The company, in its beginning, was a typical merchant house, of which Bristol, London, Liverpool or Hull would have had many counterparts. It was primarily a partnership in the leather trade, with a subsidiary house in New York, and with shipping interests at home. Here, the ownership of each vessel was also an individual partnership, administered by the common and financially predominant partner. Had the detailed records of the earlier family business in corn survived, little difference would have been found between the organization of Thomas and George Booth and that of their grandchildren between 1863-1900. At their Liverpool offices, Charles and Alfred Booth were active merchants with a minute knowledge not only of the products in which they dealt, but also of the technicalities of shipping. It was here that the finances of the two branches of the business were co-ordinated and a general supervision exercised over the American house. Even their earlier letters, with their interlardings of gossip and political news, were in the tradition of English mercantile life. The accumulation of work, the increasing intricacies of steamers and the speed and economy of telegraphy, modified this leisureliness in the later decades of the century. But neither the removal of Charles Booth to London, nor the formation of the Booth Steamship Company in 1881, caused any fundamental alteration at first. There was, of course, a stream of correspondence to and from the office of the principal partner, but the firm remained centred in Liverpool, with its work very much as it had been. The steamship company, designed to obtain additional capital, was an administrative convenience: Alfred Booth and Company remained the largest owners and it was from their offices that the steamers were managed. Here, at the end of the century, the work divided itself into three broad divisions. There was, first, the pickled pelt trade, including that from New Zealand and the buying and selling of American domestic skins: secondly, the rapidly growing business in finished leather: and lastly, the steamship company with its important agencies on the Amazon river. Each—as it has been shown—required considerable financial activity, not least being the remittances from New York to England, representing pickled pelt sales and steamer earnings, which amounted to £462,000 in 1899, £342,000 in 1900 and £354,000 in the following year.

The growth of Booth and Company in the 'nineties—with an outpost in Sydney and Christchurch, the arrangement with J. P. Mathieu and Company for the tanning of goatskins—involved an increasing devolution of management to the American partner. His position, broadly speaking, was that he proceeded without consultation as long as the business was transacted on agreed lines and in unanimity with the departmental heads: provided that constant and immediate advice be sent to Liverpool on what had taken place: and that actions involving a change of principle must have the consent of the English partners. The first steps in the creation of legally separate firms were the interests acquired in the tanneries at Nuneaton, Hitchin and Lincoln. Alfred Booth and Company continued to be the managing owners of the first Booth Steamship Company, despite its existence as an individual enterprise. The first major change came with the formation of the second Booth Steamship Company. With members of the Singlehurst family on the directorate and with a large debenture issue, this greatly enlarged branch of the business became a separate legal and managerial unit. It was a fully formed subsidiary of Alfred Booth and Company which owned all the ordinary shares. Hard on the heels of this change came two further developments. The Manáos Harbour Limited was established in 1903, although with no direct relationship to the parent company : and in the following year came the agreement with J. P. Mathieu which subsequently led to the formation of the Surpass Leather Company. Within three years, therefore, the two major interests of the firm had assumed the form of legal entities, attached through the ownership of their capital to Alfred Booth and Company.

Shorn of the responsibility for the immediate day-to-day running of its business, Alfred Booth and Company increasingly assumed the functions of an holding and banking concern. In this development, the provision of inter-company loans, the trans-Atlantic remittances of steamship and pickled pelt earnings, and the fact that London was the world's banking centre, were all important elements. Sterling credits ran, not only to India, China, and South America, from which areas goatskins were obtained, but to all parts of the world. As a consequence, credits for the Surpass Leather Company were arranged in England, between Alfred Booth and Company and Baring Brothers : the bills of exchange on Barings, London, being met by payments from Surpass to Barings' American house. Alfred Booth and Company functioned as bankers on behalf of their employees in all parts of the world. 'All our depositors,' it was stated in 1911, 'make considerable use of us as bankers, paying in and out constantly. Supplies may be bought in England, or subscriptions to clubs kept up or allowances made to family dependents, all such payments being made out of their Liverpool deposits.' In this way, it became desirable to turn the partnership into a private, limited liability company, primarily concerned with investment and banking. This occurred in June, 1914, when Alfred Booth and Company Limited was incorporated with a share capital of £1,000,000 in ordinary shares of £1 denomination. In the following year Booth and Company became a legal entity under American law, with interests in the Gardiner-Lucas Candy and Glue Company and the Densten Felt and Hair Company.

In 1919, the various American holdings, as they then existed, were financially concentrated into a trust—the Battery Company, thus providing a structure similar to that existing in England. Eighteen years later, however, the incidence of American taxation led to the winding-up of the trust, and the American organization reverted to its earlier direct relationship with the parent company. Finally, the extensions of the business in the inter-war years fell, legally, into line with the structure evolved between 1900 and 1914. In an age of highly organized business, activities which were once transacted in an ordinary merchant house under a partnership organization, now received a legal existence, a formal birth and death. To this development the growth of the business, the administrative and financial advantages of company organization, and the increasing pressure of taxation, were all contributory factors.

The new constitution of the firm did not, however, alter the fact that it remained a family business carried on fundamentally as a partnership. The capital structure was as flexible under the new as under the old arrangements. There have been accordingly a number of changes in the amount of the authorized and issued capital since 1914. In 1916, for example, the former was divided into £600,000 ordinary and £400,000 preference shares in order to meet the needs of members of the family who did not directly participate in the business. Three years later the amount of each type of share was raised to a million pounds; while in 1928 the preference shares were subdivided into first and second categories. Since that date the preference shares have been redeemed and the authorized capital today stands at two million pounds in ordinary shares. The issued capital amounting to £800,000 remained practically unchanged until 1919 and 1920 when it was twice substantially increased. The rigorous business conditions of the nine-teen-twenties led to a reduction in 1931 as the losses then in-curred were written off, and a further reduction occurred in 1939. During the war it was decided to repay the preference capital and finally the sale of the Booth Steamship Company in 1946 enabled a capital bonus to be distributed to the ordinary shareholders. The present issued capital amounts to £563,000.

One interesting consequence of this evolution of the parent company into a predominantly financial house, and of the general appearance of joint-stock organization in English busi-ness, was that the merchant partner became, what might be called, the professional director. Until the outbreak of the Great War, although in an ever smaller degree, much of the detailed, day-to-day work fell to the lot of the partners. As the twentieth century progressed, the senior members of the firm found themselves increasingly pre-occupied with the im-mediate affairs of the estate. They became concerned with problems arising from the general and financial conditions of business. As a consequence, the experience afforded by the running of a world-wide enterprise led to invitations to take part in the control of other, and often allied, enterprises. Neither Alfred nor Charles Booth held such outside appoint-ments; partly because of the narrower range of opportunities in the nineteenth century, partly because of their social and intellectual interests. It was in the second and third genera-tions of the Booth family that this became a characteristic feature. Charles Booth, the elder son of Alfred Booth, was appointed a director of the Midland Railway in 1898, and be-came its deputy-chairman in 1918, and chairman between 1919-1922. From 1916 until 1919 he was also chairman of the Bank of Liverpool. When the first of these concerns became part of the London, Midland and Scottish Railway, and the second amalgamated with Martin's Bank, he remained a director of both until his death in 1938. He was from 1924 a member of the Mersey Docks and Harbour Board, and for nineteen years chairman of the Employers' Association of the Port of Liver-pool. From 1912 until 1938 he was also chairman of the Booth Steamship Company, and of Alfred Booth and Company from 1916 to 1938. His brother, Sir Alfred Booth, Bt., became a director of the Cunard Company in 1901, its deputy-chairman in 1909-13, and chairman and managing director from 1910 to 1922. He was at various times a director of the American-Levant Company, the Anchor-Donaldson Line and of Messrs. T. and J. Brocklebank and Company, all great shipping firms. He relinquished his outside business interests in 1922 when they proved too great a strain upon his health, but remained actively concerned in the affairs of Alfred Booth and Company until his death in March, 1948. In the same way, George M. Booth, who succeeded to the chairmanship of Alfred Booth and Company in 1938, and retained the post until 1952, has undertaken wide outside responsibilities. He was a director of the Bank of England from 1915 until 1947, for many years he has been the chairman of Manáos Harbour Limited, and still is on the board of White Drummond and Company, the Municipal and General Securities Ltd., and Manáos Tramways and Light Company. Until it was taken over by the Brazilian Government, he was for a considerable time director, and later chairman, of the important São Paulo Railway Company; and from 1942 until 1945 chairman of the Brazilian Chamber of Commerce and Economic Affairs.

This interest in affairs outside the family business has been continued in the third generation by the present chairman, John Wells Booth. Mr Booth was for some years a director of the Cunard Steamship Company and later held high office in British South-American Airways and British Overseas Airways until his return in 1950 to Alfred Booth and Company in a full-time capacity. He remains a director of British Overseas Airways Corporation and of the Phoenix Insurance Company.

CHAPTER XIV

Alfred Booth and Company Today

―――――

Alfred Booth and Company is an outstanding, but by no means unique, example of the development of the family firm. Similar private concerns can be found in most branches of business, some with a continuous history covering two hundred years and more. Although the company cannot claim such longevity, being still in its tenth decade and with only the third generation of partners, yet its story is typical of this form of enterprise. Like others of its kind, Alfred Booth and Company originated in, and still retains many of the more pleasant features of, the 'old industry'—a 'curious blend of discipline and good nature, fairmindedness and competition'. Like others of its kind too, it has shown a remarkable degree of adaptation to changes in its economic environment, involving a continual growth and decay of the company's individual activities. Where, perhaps, the firm has been somewhat unusual, is in the range of its interests, for at one stage they encompassed merchanting, shipowning, tanning, building and, to some extent, financing. Had English civil aviation remained entirely in private ownership, yet another item might well have been added to this list.

As events have turned out, the changes of the last ten years have tended to reduce the range of the company's interests while maintaining the extent of its business. In England, the most important feature of this process of change has been the withdrawal from shipowning. In America, the firm has ceased to be manufacturers with the sale of the Surpass Leather Company's factory and the Densten Felt and Hair Company, and has reverted to its former occupation as suppliers of leather and raw-stock for the American light leather industry. In this way, the company's original status as an international merchant house has been maintained. There are agents who buy goat-skins in the African, Brazilian, Indian, and Chinese markets. This part of the company's activities is strengthened by the work of the long-established raw-stock agencies in Australasia. The Sydney office of Booth and Company, for example, was responsible for 42 per cent. of the total exports from Australia of kangaroo skins in 1946, and 72 per cent. in 1950.

On the other hand, the last decade has witnessed an increased investment in the English enterprises of Alfred Booth and Company. Its two largest manufacturing units on this side of the Atlantic are now the Pavlova Leather Company and B. Cannon and Company. The first of these, with its sports-field, occupies thirty-five acres of land at Abingdon, Berkshire. Here, nearly two hundred men and women are employed in turning New Zealand sheep and lamb pelts, African and Argentinian goat-skins, Brazilian, East African and Indian hair-sheepskins into leather, finished mainly on the flesh or 'suede' side. The eventual destination of these products is the manufacture of shoes, gloves and clothes: some of the skins are, however, split, and the grain side tanned to make leather for bookbind-ings, bag linings and fancy goods. Experiments have also been undertaken here in the production of Beaver Lamb for the fur trade. The products of the works of B. Cannon and Company at Lincoln are gelatine, glue and concentrated size. The raw materials for these important products are drawn, in the main, from the waste material of various English tanneries; although some is imported from abroad, particularly 'osseine', a highly concentrated gelatinous product made from bones. A cold water paste for the decorating trade is made, while grease, obtained as a by-product, has also commanded a ready sale.

The firm of Wade and Company (Nottingham), in which Alfred Booth and Company have a substantial interest, pro-duces Glacé kid and suede with an output of some 1,600 dozen skins weekly. A newly-formed subsidiary of this company, the Charles Tanneries Ltd., acts as selling agent for the products of the factory both in England and in Europe, together with some of the other kinds of leather made by the Booths.

Perhaps the most interesting development on this side of the business during the post-war years has been the venture into the making of hide leather, begun in 1948 with the purchase of a small tannery at Beverley, Yorkshire. During the first years the weekly output amounted to 350 hides, produced from South American and African raw-stock tanned in old-fashioned pits with vegetable agents. The plant and buildings have now been modernized and extended, and pit tanning has been replaced by machines and chemicals. In addition to the sole and insole leather thus produced, experiments have been made in the manufacture of shell cordovan leather, which, according to one member of the firm, 'resembles a beautiful piece of timber, as unequalled as a Stradivarius violin, which should only be played by and to people who appreciate fullness and lasting beauty'.

Developments in the English leather business have been paralleled by the growth of the Unit Construction Company, which is now the largest element in the Booth organization. With branches in London, Liverpool and Belfast, it directly employs 3,500 men, in addition to nearly a thousand in the pay of various sub-contractors. The company's turnover of business amounted to £4,465,000 in 1950 and has increased since that date.

TABLE X

UNIT CONSTRUCTION COMPANY

YEARLY CASH TURNOVER

1947 (15 months)	£2,603,000	1952	£6,590,000
1948	£3,511,000	1953	£7,550,000
1949	£4,070,000	1954	£6,119,000
1950	£4,465,000	1955	£5,367,000
1951	£5,332,000	1956	£6,075,000
		1957	£6,420,000

In these eleven years building to the value of some fifty-eight million pounds has been undertaken, of which about a quarter represents value of contracts financed by the London County Council. Each of the branches has been engaged on large re-housing schemes—at Speke, Kirkby, Oxhey, Aveley and Bracknell: while flats have been built at Battersea, Camberwell, and Stockwell, and houses, roads and sewers in Northern Ireland. The growth of the business has led to three important developments within the company. The increase of the staff has led to far-reaching apprenticeship training schemes—an extension of the old Booth tradition into a new sphere; to the establishment of sport and benefit clubs at the various branches; and to the appointment of welfare officers on the sites of the major contracts. Secondly the Pierhead Ltd. of Liverpool was established in 1946 as a subsidiary, originally to supply the Unit Construction Company with reinforced and pre-stressed concrete joists, tiles, blocks and slabs. Today, with a branch at Feltham, this highly successful project sells its products generally to the building industry. Finally, a research department has been created with the object, not only of testing new materials and machinery, but of devising methods of increasing productivity. Associated with this department has been the interest taken in aluminium sheet as a building material. This originated in arrangements made with Costains and Company and Sir Robert McAlpine and Company in 1946 to erect the 'Orlit' type of house under contract with the Ministry of Supply. Since then, the company has developed a variety of temporary and pre-fabricated houses from this and other materials, which have been extensively used in this country and in the tropics. Of these, the 'Ubique', the 'Ditton', and the 'Uniport Altent'—the last designed by T. G. Randolph, until recently secretary of the Unit Construction Company—are typical examples.

Thus, with its creditable record of adaptation and achievement, Alfred Booth and Company moves into its second century.

THE BOOTH STEAMSHIP COMPANY
THE FLEET 1865–1946

Ship	Year built	Builders	Dimensions in feet			Registered Tonnage		Engines	Nominal H.P.	Period with fleet
			L'gth	B'th	W'th	Gross	Net			
Augustine	1865	Hart & Sinnot, Liverpool	213.5	29.6	25.1	1106	814	Comp'd Inverted	95	1865–1892
Jerome	1865	,,	213.8	29.7	25.3	1090	796	,,	91	1865–1890
Ambrose	1869	Hawthorn Leslie, Newcastle	242.0	29.6	24.7	1168	756	Compound	90	1869–1894
Bernard	1870	Royden & Sons, Liverpool	237.2	26.2	19.9	915	577	Com'd Inverted	90	1870–1889
Basil	1871	Scott, Greenock	221.4	30.4	17.6	1185	748	,,	120	1882–1897
Anselm	1882	Hawthorn Leslie, Newcastle	271.0	33.8	22.9	1562	998	Compound	140	1882–1898
Clement	1877	Cammell Laird, Birkenhead	230.4	31.1	19.6	1227	785	Com'd Inverted	150	1883–1897
Lanfranc	1884	Royden & Sons, Liverpool	280.9	34.2	22.9	1657	1070	Compound	138	1884–1898
Cyril	1882	London & Glasgow Co.	235.0	31.3	17.1	1190	751	Com'd Inverted	130	1884–1897
Gregory	1879	Schlesinger Davis, Newcastle	253.0	33.0	16.9	1571	1002	Compound	142	1880–1897
Justin	1880	Hall & Co., Aberdeen	278.0	34.4	22.9	1744	1124	,,	200	1890–1898
Origen	1886	Hall Russell, Aberdeen	250.6	34.6	22.7	1612	1034	Triple Expansion	170	1891–1899
Hilary	1889	Thompson, Dundee	275.0	37.2	15.9	1930	1251	,,	180	1892–1905
Hildebrand	1893	Hall Russell, Aberdeen	260.3	36.2	23.4	1947	1224	,,	200	1893–1908
Hubert	1894	Hall Russell, Aberdeen	261.4	36.2	17.7	1922	1211	,,	200	1894–1908
Dunstan	1895	Barclay, Curle, Glasgow	322.0	42.3	16.9	2966	1893	,,	277	1895–1923
Dominic	1895	Barclay, Curle, Glasgow	322.0	42.3	16.9	2966	1893	,,	277	1895–1923
Horatio	1892	Edwards S.B. Co., Newcastle	331.0	40.2	19.1	3212	2078	,,	287	1895–1911
Augustine	1879	Barclay, Curle, Glasgow	359.6	43.8	29.1	3498	2192	,,	508	1896–1912
Polycarp	1896	Barclay, Curle, Glasgow	322.0	42.3	16.9	2966	1893	,,	277	1896–1912
Benedict	1894	Raylton Dixon, Middlesb.	345.0	43.5	25.3	2440	1681	,,	334	1897–1924
Jerome	1877	Napier & Sons, Glasgow	348.9	39.4	28.8	3056	1880	,,	435	1897–1910
Bernard	1895	Workman Clark, Belfast	335.0	43.7	18.2	3280	2116	,,	292	1895–1911
Basil	1895	Workman Clark, Belfast	338.0	43.7	26.1	3223	2092	,,	334	1898–1917
Gregory	1891	Palmer's, Newcastle	256.0	40.0	15.9	2030	1287	,,	222	1899–1920
Clement	1896	Napier & Sons, Glasgow	345.7	44.1	24.6	3445	2166	,,	441	1900–1914
Cyril	1883	G. Elder & Co., Glasgow	280.6	48.2	31.4	4380	2556	,,	831	1902–1905
Ambrose	1902	Raylton, Dixon Middlesb.	375.2	47.8	18.5	4187	2128	,,	775	1902–1915

Ship	Year built	Builders	Dimensions in feet			Registered Tonnage		Engines	Nominal H.P.	Period with fleet
			L'gth	B'th	W'th	Gross	Net			
Boniface	1904	Barclay, Curle & Co., Glasgow	355.0	48.7	24.0	3506	2256	Triple Expansion	400	1904–1917
Justin	1904	„	255.0	48.7	24.0	3890	2424	„	400	1094–1930
Anselm	1905	Workman, Clark & Co. Belfast	400.4	50.1	19.1	5442	3213	„	819	1905–1922
Cuthbert	1906	Hawthorn Leslie, Newcastle	355.1	49.3	23.9	3563	2274	„	409	1906–1931
Anthony	1907	„	418.5	52.3	27.2	6439	3753	„	850	1907–1917
Lanfranc	1907	Caledon S.B.&E.Co., Dundee	418.5	52.2	27.3	6275	3655	„	850	1907–1917
Crispin	1907	Raylton Dixon & Co., Middlesb.	355.1	49.3	24.1	3694	2304	„	408	1907–1917
Hilary	1908	Caledon S.B.&E.Co., Dundee	418.5	52.2	27.3	6325	3626	„	848	1907–1917
Francis	1910	Barclay Curle & Co., Glasgow	355.0	49.2	24.2	3960	2512	„	401	1910–1931
Hubert	1910	„	355.0	49.2	24.2	3930	2486	„	401	1910–1934
Christopher	1910	Tyne I.S.B. Co., Newcastle	360.0	50.1	22.8	4143	2576	„	367	1910–1915
Stephen	1910	Hawthorn Leslie, Newcastle	375.5	50.3	23.6	4444	2799	„		1910–1935
Vincent	1910	Mackie, Thompson, Glasgow	180.7	33.1	15.3	986	571	„	108	1910–1933
Denis	1911	Hawthorn, Leslie, Newcastle	376.4	50.3	23.6	4435	2807	„	446	1911–1932
Aidan	1911	Tyne I.S.B.Co., Newcastle	375.9	50.3	23.5	4545	2863	„	456	1911–1934
Hildebrand	1911	Scotts S.B.&E.Co., Greenock	440.3	54.1	27.3	6991	4245	Quadruple Expn.	946	1911–1932
Pancras	1911	Hawthorn Leslie, Newcastle	376.3	50.3	23.6	4436	2809	Triple Expansion	446	1911–1933
Alban	1914	Caledon S.B.&E.Co., Dundee	375.2	51.7	29.7	5223	3262	„	466	1914–1935
Michael	1914	Raylton Dixon, Middlesboro	300.5	45.3	25.7	3172	1938	„	306	1914–1924
Polycarp	1918	Barclay, Curle & Co., Glasgow	340.7	46.8	25.6	3577	2249	„	403	1918–1940
Origen	1918	Caledon S.B.&E.Co., Dundee	340.6	46.7	25.6	3545	2214	„	388	1918–1918
Dominic	1922	Krupps, Kiel	290.2	46.8	26.6	3396	2081	„	338	1927–1932
Dunstan	1925	Duncan & Co., Glasgow	404.9	53.0	27.6	5149	3266	„	477	1935–1941
Basil	1928	Hawthorn Leslie, Newcastle	407.9	53.8	26.0	4873	3030	„	600	1928–1946
Boniface	1928	„	407.8	53.8	26.0	4877	3030	„	668	1928–1946
Benedict	1930	„	408.5	53.7	26.0	4920	2980	„	608	1930–1946
Hilary	1931	Cammell Laird, Birkenhead	424.2	56.2	34.2	7403	4350	„	1033	1931–1946
Clement	1934	„	412.2	55.7	26.0	5051	3082	„	652	1934–1939
Crispin	1935	„	412.2	55.7	26.0	5051	3082	„	603	1935–1941
Anselm	1935	Denny & Bros., Dumbarton	412.3	55.7	25.8	5954	3609	„	696	1935–1944

THE BOOTH STEAMSHIP COMPANY

SHIPS ACQUIRED FROM THE RED CROSS LINE IN 1901

Ship	Year Built	Builders	Dimensions in feet			Registered Tonnage		Engines	Nominal H.P.	Period with fleet
			L'th	B'th	W'th	Gross	Net			
Lisbonense	1871	T. Royden & Sons, Liverpool	269.4	33.2	16.4	1657	1051	Triple Expansion	201	1901–1903
Paraense	1871	,,	270.2	33.0	28.9	1697	1094	,,	202	1901–1902
Sobralense	1884	Barrow Steam Boat Co.	275.1	34.2	23.5	1982	1232	,,	233	1901–1904
Maranhense	1890	Caird & Co., Greenock	313.6	42.1	24.1	2767	1784	,,	310	1901–1909
Fluminense	1891	Palmer & Co., Newcastle	302.0	38.4	15.3	2154	1275	,,	428	1901–1909
Madeirense	1891	Bonn & Mees, Rotterdam	332.0	40.0	22.6	2831	1662	,,	500	1901–1910
Camtense	1891	Palmer Co., Newcastle	302.0	38.4	15.3	2184	1314	,,	428	1901–1909
Obidense	1891	T. Royden & Sons, Liverpool	300.0	37.1	23.4	2380	1511	,,	414	1901–1910
Cearense	1891	Naval Con. & Arm. Co., Barrow	318.0	40.4	25.8	2769	1790	,,	283	1901–1911
Grangense	1892	Palmers Co., Newcastle	302.0	38.4	15.3	2162	1244	,,	428	1901–1910
Amazonense	1899	D. J. Dunlop & Co., Glasgow	312.0	40.9	17.6	2828	1859	,,	243	1901–1911

THE BOOTH IQUITOS STEAMSHIP COMPANY
(Later amalgamated with the B.S.S. Co.)

Ship	Year built	Builders	Dimensions in feet			Registered Tonnage		Engines	Nominal H.P.	Period with fleet
			L'th	B'th	W'th	Gross	Net			
Huascar	1896	Sunderland S.B. Co.	215.0	31.1	14.6	875	532	Triple Expansion	113	1896–1908
Bolivar	1898	Hall Russell, Aberdeen	223.0	33.1	15.5	1016	615	,,		1899–1909
Huayana (ex Hildebrand, built in 1893. see ante)										
Atahualpa	1894	Hall Russell, Aberdeen	261.4	36.2	17.7	1965	1233	,,	194	1908–1919
Manco	1908	Scotts S.B.&E.Co., Greenock	300.3	45.2	21.1	2979	1826	,,	381	1908–1921

SHIPS ACQUIRED FROM THE RED CROSS IQUITOS COMPANY, 1902

Ship	Year built	Builders	Dimensions in feet			Registered Tonnage		Engines	Nominal H.P.	Period with fleet
			L'th	B'th	W'th	Gross	Net			
Napo	1897	S.P. Austin, Sunderland	224.4	33.4	13.8	1091	663	Triple Expansion	156	1901–1913
Javary	1898		235.5	34.3	14.5	1249	783	,,	156	1901–1914
Ucayali	1898	Wood, Skinner, '', Newcastle	230.0	32.2	14.2	1052	574	,,	186	1901–1914

INDEX

N

GEORGE ALLEN & UNWIN LTD
London: 40 Museum Street, W.C.1

Auckland: 24 Wyndham Street
Bombay: 15 Graham Road, Ballard Estate, Bombay 1
Calcutta: 17 Chittaranjan Avenue, Calcutta 13
Cape Town: 109 Long Street
Karachi: Metherson's Estate, Wood Street, Karachi 2
New Delhi: 13-14 Ajmeri Gate Extension, New Delhi 1
Sao Paulo: Avenida 9 de Julho 1138-Ap. 51
Singapore, South East Asia & Far East, 36c, Princep Street
Sydney, N.S.W.: Bradbury House, 55 York Street
Toronto: 91 Wellington Street West

For Product Safety Concerns and Information please contact our EU
representative GPSR@taylorandfrancis.com
Taylor & Francis Verlag GmbH, Kaufingerstraße 24, 80331 München, Germany

www.ingramcontent.com/pod-product-compliance
Lightning Source LLC
Chambersburg PA
CBHW061200220326
41599CB00025B/4551

*9 7 8 1 1 3 8 8 6 5 1 2 9 *